Tensions in the Performance of Music

Acknowledgments
The editor wishes to thank all the contributors; also Joseph Bloch, Dr. Mosco Carner and Ronald Stevenson for their encouragement and Gretchen Nelson and Nicholas Devon for their constructive suggestions; but above all our students without whom these studies would not have been possible.

Tensions in the Performance of Music

A Symposium Edited by Carola Grindea
Foreword by Yehudi Menuhin
Preface by Allen Percival

Kahn & Averill, London

Pro/Am Music Resources Inc, White Plains, New York

This extended edition first published in 1995 by
Kahn & Averill
9 Harrington Road, London SW7 3ES

British Library Cataloguing in Publication Data
A catalogue record for this book is available from the British Library

ISBN 1 871082 59 5

This edition first published in the United States in 1995 by
Pro/Am Music Resources Inc
63 Prospect Street, White Plains, New York 10606

ISBN 0-912483-71-7 (USA)

Printed in Great Britain by
Redwood Books, Trowbridge, Wilts

Contents

Foreword

In normal life the distance between the dream and its fulfilment is a very long one; indeed the dream may never be fulfilled; but in the case of an artist in top form the dream and fulfilment are simultaneous. At that moment there is no tension. In this respect musicians are blessed. However, a very great number do not reach this stage; some of the obstacles seem insurmountable and perhaps many of them, if not most, lie within the potential capacity of the performing musician to overcome. We have intensely to want and to wish yet to behave as if we did not; the more determined we are, the more patient and untense we must learn to be. Wanting and wishing alone will not bring results.

In all the articles contained in this book the reader will notice how important are the attributes of patience, persistence, self-awareness and above all the attitude of humble searching, rewarding discovery. At the same time he will notice the total absence of the narrow ambitious ego. Some people may successfully combine consuming ambition and cold method but the ambition of serving and yielding, of perfection, elegance and economy, of serenity of purpose and execution, these are surely the highest aims we can envisage. I hope and pray that each reader will glean from this book a few ideas which will help him along the way of inner happiness and enhanced capacity.

Yehudi Menuhin
London, July 1977

Preface

Tension — physical and mental — is of course part of the human condition. But for the performing artist in music, drama or dance, tension plays perhaps a disproportionate part in normal, everyday life. In these short articles, Carola Grindea has collected a fascinating variety of views on what should, can and may be done to avoid the evil effects of conflicting tensions. Those writing as instrumentalists are naturally greatly concerned with relieving physical tension and achieving the muscular co-ordination essential to technical competence; the two teachers of voice production emphasize the need to relax even in performance; for the conductor and the composer, the tension is in the music and subject to rigorous mental tensions before its creation; for the specialist in Alexander Technique, too, the prime importance is preparation and the essential is self-discovery.

Yet time and again the authors overlap, quite unwittingly, to reveal that Carola Grindea's self-confessed 'obsession' with the problems of tension is not an eccentricity but a true concern to learn from twentieth-century life how to cope with them, learning from the past, from other cultures, from developing science and from fellow-artists. I have been privileged to know almost all the contributors as my colleagues at the Guildhall School of Music and Drama. The attributes found by Yehudi Menuhin in reading their articles are indeed those of a group of artists who, coming from different schools of training and from many countries, dedicate themselves to the future of the professions they serve.

Allen Percival
Principal: Guildhall School
of Music and Drama
London, August 1977

Introduction
Carola Grindea

The problems created by *tensions in the performance of music* have been almost an obsession with me for some time. I tried to discuss them with a number of musicians, to find out their views, how they approach these problems and what was their attitude towards their students' difficulties. Mostly, however, I hoped to get some valid comments which could give me an insight into the complexities created by this constant and mysterious companion of our lives.

I was confronted with varied and quite surprising answers.

"I never mention the word *tension*. It is bad psychology," was one of the replies.

' If any of my students haven't got it, I certainly *give* it to them! '

Or, from another colleague: "Surely, my students' playing reflects my ability to cope with this *and* other problems."

In fact they were all quite right. It is sometimes 'bad psychology' to emphasise a negative aspect of a student's work. Instead, this teacher believed that by helping him with the technical difficulties, he hoped to get the right results. Confidence and sense of achievement are certainly the best substitute for fear or anxiety.

In the same way, 'if they haven't got it, I certainly give it to them' is almost a 'cri de coeur', the most natural reaction of a fine performer who expects deep emotional response from the student confronted with a great work. This artist was doing his best to get him more involved, as everyone knows how dull a performance lacking in intensity can be.

Indeed, the many replies to my queries reflected the attitude of serious musicians who, either instinctively or through long teaching experience, were confident that their way of handling their students' problems was the right one

However, I was looking for more positive guidance into this highly sensitive area of exploration. Searching the libraries I found indeed a number of interesting books on the subject written by eminent psychologists, but they treated this topic from a clinical aspect.

While studying treatises on Piano Technique, I was interested to read that the term *tension* was used by most great pedagogues, from Girolamo Diruta in one of the earliest published texts, to C. P. E. Bach, Beethoven, Mozart, Hummel and many others, when referring to the conditions of the hands in piano playing. It is only since the 'relaxionists' introduced what they thought was the antidote to tension, 'relaxation in piano playing', that a new phraseology was launched. This dominated a good part of the first half of this century, until new theories and experiments proved that there cannot be relaxation in the performance of music, and the old cliché — tension — is now back into the terminology of piano technique.

I am convinced that a study of *tensions in the performance of music* presenting various approaches, is greatly needed. Hence this symposium, in which several contributors, who have given a great deal of thought to this real and serious problem confronting the performing musician, have been free to express their views, no matter how contradictory. I believe this exploratory attempt to be the first study of its kind, and we hope that it will stimulate others to go further and, perhaps, find new paths towards better solutions to these mysterious and so often incomprehensible phenomena. We also hope that most of us *will stop creating so much tension while exploring ways and means to get rid of it!*

KATÓ HAVAS

The Release from Tension and Anxiety in String Playing

Tension and anxiety are part of us all to a larger or smaller degree; so are fear, the desire to be loved, and a feeling of guilt. The need to eliminate, or at least to overcome these anxieties, often creates such a strong stimulus in people that it becomes the very source of their creative motivation.

As all performers know, nobody plays the same in public as he does alone. One plays either much better or much worse. When the audience acts as a stimulus to the performer, so that he can release his inborn anxiety through his playing, the performance usually becomes sparkling and exciting. But when the anxieties are exaggerated before an audience and the player knows that he is unable to communicate the music, it is then that neuroses set in. If this becomes a regular occurence the player sometimes ends up with a nervous breakdown.

Alas, as so many musicians know to their cost, there are few activities in life which can produce tension and anxiety as rapidly and thoroughly as playing a musical instrument in public. And it seems that the classical violinist is one of the hardest hit. I specify 'classical' because while the Hungarian gypsy fiddler creates a feeling of well-being and of having a good time as a matter of course, the conventional violinist is usually beset with so many problems that his playing often deteriorates into a matter of sheer physical survival. (This is in spite of the fact that he has probably put in

many more hours of hard work than most other musicians). On the other hand the gypsy (and those are
usually the best) has often never had a formal lesson in
his life, let alone those hours of practice. "It came
quite natural" to quote my old friend and childhood
hero, Csicso, the Hungarian Gypsy[1].

It is also interesting to note that the legendary
players who have transcended their instruments with
the magic of their music (like Kreisler and Rubinstein,
to name but two) are well known for never having
practised. But what few people realize is that both these
artists in fact worked very hard, not with their hands,
but with their heads. Kreisler, for example, was said
to have memorized a concerto on the train between
one big city and another, and then to have played it
with the orchestra without any previous practice on the
violin. But these giants are rare in the classical world.
In *Stage Fright, Its Causes and Cures* I have devoted
a whole chapter to discussing the Hungarian gypsy
violinists, because their virtuosity, ease and dexterity
of technique, the warmth and infinite variety of their
tone colouring, their power of musical communication,
are novel phenomena rarely matched by any classical
violinist. The question is, why?

Before seeking the causes of the vast difference
between these two types of players — those who work
hard on the violin, exuding a lot of effort, and those
who know how to 'let the music happen' with ease
and pleasure — it is perhaps worth assessing just what
music-making is supposed to be all about.

We all know that music is one of the most basic
forms of human communication, from the most primitive tribes to the (so-called) civilized societies of the
world. Among primitive men we may not find books
and paintings, but there is always music in some form
or other. In fact they often consider music to be the
only fundamental link with the unknown powers.

Some scientists have actually produced evidence that music has a profound effect on all living things, animal and vegetable alike. According to Aristotle, music not only portrays the outward appearance of human feeling and action, but also represents the inner significance of emotional life, of man's moods and activities, more effectively than other arts. So, with all this power of universal communication at his disposal, why does a classical violinist find it so difficult actually to communicate, very often quite impossible, to 'give' at all?

The inability to communicate is certainly not due to a lack of desire to do so, or a lack of ability, or of talent (as has so often been proved to me by violinists I have worked with), but it is the result of physical tensions, faulty mental attitudes, and social pressures. Whether it is the physical tensions which create the faulty mental attitudes, or the faulty mental attitudes that create the physical tensions is as difficult to answer as the question as to which came first, the chicken or the egg. One thing is certain: that while the social pressures are a separate problem, albeit a considerable one, the physical and mental aspects of violin playing are so interrelated that it is impossible to separate them. As the physical tensions are more obvious than the faulty mental attitudes, and are therefore easier to clarify, let us begin with them.

We all know that every form of art depends on movement and flow. But while this movement and flow can be retained forever in a painting or in the written word, it can never be captured in music. Music is the only art form which is a perpetual 'fluid flow'. And this is the first problem that we face when we play an instrument. Because to realize this 'fluid flow' on an instrument which feels hard to the touch is very difficult indeed, even in the best of circumstances. For the hard texture of the instrument tends to create a static (if not equally hard) response in the hands. This static response causes

tensions, and tensions create anxiety. This is a particularly special problem for the violinist because the
tensions resulting from static hands can affect his whole
body to such an extent that he is completely unable
to release his musical imagination. This can become a
very \serious problem in time, with far-reaching consequences. And no wonder, when all our activities, no
matter how ordinary, in fact our very existence, depend
on an interrelated and harmonious mobility which
transmits energy. In a human being this transmission
of energy release is always an 'inside-outward' process.
For example, an enthusiastic greeting usually takes
the form of a person throwing his arms open and
outwards to emphasize the meaning of his 'Hello, I am
glad to see you'. This gesture of, 'Hello, I am glad to
see you' would not be half as powerful if the arms
were hampered by stiff joints. If the joints were completely blocked by tensions and could not open at
all, the greeting would be so enfeebled by the lack of
energy transference that it would lose its purpose
altogether.

Besides the hard texture of the instrument, there
are two other major causes which block the 'inside-
outward' flow of energy transference. One is the violin
and bow 'hold'. This is often manifested by an inward
twist of the left elbow to help *hold* the violin and a
hard grip in the right-hand fingers to help *hold* the
bow. The second is the fact that the eyes fall on the
hands of the player. As the function of the eyes is to
inform the nervous system about the world around us,
we naturally act according to their information, and
obey their commands without question. 'But I saw it
with my own eyes' is the expression we often use
when we want to prove something. Because in violin
playing the focus is on the left-hand fingertips, it
seems inevitable to the player that he must twist his
left hand towards the fingerboard so that the fingers

can reach over to 'hit', 'hammer', or at least to 'stop'
the notes on the string, especially when playing on the
G string. Also, from the point of view of the eyes,
it seems obvious that it is the right wrist and fingers
that manipulate the bow. Thus begins the grind of
practising the left-hand techniques to strengthen and
stretch the fingers, with the additional right wrist and
finger exercises to 'push' and 'pull' the bow. The result
is a very forcible negation of the power of the 'inside-
outward' energy transference. Owing to the three major
causes of physical tensions just discussed, there are
countless other forces pulling against each other within
the player, inducing effort in the movements and conflict in the mind. So the concept that the violin is a
very difficult instrument to play is inevitable. But
again this concept is only one of many faulty attitudes.
Another one is the 'vertical' attitude of playing; i.e.,
the downward pressure of the head on the chin-rest,
and the downward pressure of the fingers on the fingerboard and on the bow. Add to this the pull of gravity
on both the arms and the violin, and the static feeling
of earthboundness which so many violinists encounter,
is complete.

In order to appreciate the full significance of this
particular faulty attitude, let us return to the question
of what music-making is all about. If music as a form of
art depends on a constant flow of movement, the
power of the inner energy that generates this flow
cannot be aimed in a downward, vertical direction.
Because even a pendulum will come to a halt when its
horizontal impulses cease to exist. It is a good thing
to remember that the flight of a bird is always horizontal, and that the proverbial 'hello' would soon lose
its impact if the arms were flung downwards, instead
of an inside-outward horizontal swing.

A third faulty attitude in violin playing is the concept (which so often prevails) that it is the bow which

decides the interpretation. This is a perfectly valid idea *if* the left hand is static because of its twisted position towards the fingerboard. For *something* must move when playing music, and the bow at least does that. But the bow cannot produce the notes themselves, let alone the shifts, double stops, trills, etc.. In fact, it is unable to create the very essence of music-making, which is the interval progression. So, owing to these three major causes of physical tension (the Wood, the Hold, and the Eyes), and owing to the three major causes of mental anxieties (the vertical concept of playing, the bow arm initiating the interpretation, and the concept that violin playing is difficult), the poor performer is so hemmed in, is so frustrated, that sometimes it seems like a miracle that anybody plays at all. But why does a gypsy not encounter these difficulties, and how is it possible for a classical violinist to eliminate them?

First of all, the gypsy is mobile. His instinct demands movement. His energy transference through the rhythmic pulse is phenomenal. He does not 'hold' the violin and bow. In fact, his head is often completely off the chin-rest, while his left hand is in a horizontal and mobile embrace *under* the fingerboard. He never looks at his hands, because he is too busy looking at the people he is playing for, to make sure they are receiving his music. As a result, he never plays externally with his hands alone, his hands are there only to follow through the inner energy (rhythmic impulses). Because he instinctively realizes the dramatic significance of the internal swings, a gypsy always leads with his left hand. He connects the intervals with a caressing, slantwise finger movement, instead of hitting the fingerboard from above. And his bow strokes are only reflex actions following the lead of the left hand.

So the first thing we must understand is that a self-generating and free-flowing inside-outward drive is *essential* to music-making in general and to violin playing in particular. We must also realize that this can only be achieved if every joint in the body is in *constant motion*. Only constant, co-ordinated motion can actively transmit the energy impulses in the form of the rhythmic pulse. *This includes the movements of the knee joints as well.*[2]

However, in order to achieve this constant and co-ordinated motion the desire to move with the body is not enough. Of course we all feel the need to move when playing. But the tendency to overwork the movements in the visible joints by wilful exercise (i.e., the wrist and finger joints in both hands) to compensate for the stiffness of the hidden joints (the shoulder joints and the arm sockets) is evident in many players. In other words, if we break the shoulder joints we cannot move the arm at all. But if we break the wrist the arm can still move quite easily. Or, for example, many violinists feel obliged to turn their bodies left and right while playing, to compensate for the stiffness in their knees. So it is of paramount importance to realize that the secret of freedom and ease is not a question of how many hours we practice, straining, often forcing the fingers to find the notes. The secret lies in the discovery of what motivates our self-propelled actions in our ordinary, everyday life, when we are not playing the violin, and then to apply the same self-propelled movements when we do play.

It is interesting to note that while the gypsy violinists, or for that matter the country fiddler and jazz player, flex their knees to 'drive the pulse' as a matter of course, many classical violinists are quite unable to move their knees at all while playing, though the knees are the greatest motivators of the rhythmic pulse. However, it must be emphasized that the natural co-ordination of self-propelled actions which we take for granted in everyday activities, can be achieved only by

specific and systematic application when it is related
to violin playing.

Due to the conflict of physical tensions and mental
anxieties so many violinists encounter, a state of inner
chaos is almost inevitable when performing. The doubt
about one's ability is there anyhow, and there is nothing
like a state of chaos to put this feeling of inadequacy
out of all proportion. Therefore the purpose of the
New Approach to Violin Playing is to ensure the differ-
entiations between causes and effects, and that all the
exercises relating to it stand for the bringing of order
into chaos and safety into uncertainty. Every artist
knows that only out of order can there be true freedom. It is important that the concept of 'order' is not
confused with discipline.[3]

Also, as it is essential for the mind and body to work
in harmony, the usage of words relating to violin playing
is as important as the exercises themselves. For example,
the word 'hold' has quite the opposite meaning to the
word 'flow'. So how can one possibly flow with the
music and 'hold' the violin at the same time? Or again,
how can the idea of 'hitting' the notes on the fingerboard, and the 'pressing' of the fingers on the bow be
reconciled with the concept of musical communication
or with the flow of the rhythmic impulses?

Although it is not possible, in this essay, to outline
the whole course of the systematic practice, a few
salient points may prove of some help.

The first, as with any other instrument, is the 'posture',
the 'stance'. In order to establish constant motion and
balance throughout the body, set the legs apart 'like
a sailor on a ship's deck'[4] and imagine that you have
a third leg behind, continuing from the base of the
spine, which is made of coils of springs. Settle into a
continuous rhythmic pulse with a slight sitting and
rising motion on your imaginary springy third leg, as
if riding a horse. This will cause the knees to bend as

a matter of course. *Sing* the piece you are working on while 'riding' the pulse, accompanying it with a rhythmic clap of the hands as well. 'Few violinists realize that singing (with the rhythmic pulse) away from their instruments, is one of the greatest releases from tension and anxiety in violin playing, apart from being the *real* inner source of their musical impulses'.[5] Another important procedure is to eliminate the 'violin hold' altogether. As I said before, many players find it quite impossible to play while their heads are off the violin. This is because it is a generally accepted fact that the violin is heavy, and unless the head holds it tightly against the shoulder, the violin will drop. Now, as any vertical pressure must have a counter-pressure, the more the head presses down into the chin-rest, the more the shoulder will have to press upward, causing the arm socket to be locked and stiff, not to mention the serious neck, back, and arm aches that often result from this.

Few violinists are able to realize that violin playing is in fact very easy and *can* be totally effortless. When it is tense and effortful it is because *we make it so,* albeit with the best intentions in the world.

For example, take hold of your violin with the left hand, with the thumb placed on the chin-rest while the fingers support it underneath. Hold it in front of you like this for a few minutes, level with the floor. It will seem very heavy indeed and will cause acute discomfort all through your arm. This is what we often experience in the real violin hold, the pull of the dead weight of the instrument in front of us. Rest a second, then open your left hand with the palm turned upwards in a straight line with the fingers. Place the middle back of the violin gently upon your palm and you will see how incredibly light it really is. It is quite astonishing. It hardly seems to weigh more than a letter. Needless to say, this is the *true weight* of the violin. The other weight, when it seems so heavy, is a result of bad posture and distorted balances. The question is not what is a good violin hold and what is a bad one. The idea is to create a feeling through co-ordinated motion and balance that there is *no violin hold at all*. So it can remain as weightless as when it rests on the palm of one's hand. This can be achieved only when we realize the 'enormous difference between the two concepts of *lifting* or *suspending* the arm'.[6]

Many players mistake the hanging of the arms in violin playing as a sign of lightness, when in fact the gravity of the earth soon makes them feel even heavier than they really are. While, when they are suspended in a horizontal flight, with arms and wrists flexed, they feel completely weightless. It is always a wonderful moment to see the players' face light up when he first experiences the feeling of having 'no arms' and 'no violin'. Children love the image of the tiny wings flying from the 'F' holes because it helps them to understand that they do not have to hold the violin as we understand it.

The same happens with the right arm, for the suspension of the upper right arm eliminates the 'bow hold' as well. While the horizontally directed rhythmic impulses of the arm socket and elbow joint ensure that the bow itself becomes only a follow-through of these impulses and is not a cumbersome, heavy object one has somehow to manipulate. Once the interrelated rhythmic division of the arm and bow are amalgamated in a whole, the detaché, spiccato, martelé, etc. become part of this co-ordinated unity, and do not need to be practised as separate entities.[7]

The best illustrations of this happened once by accident. At a workshop in the United States, when I felt the weight of the bow as I was illustrating the spiccato, I put it down to an off day on my part, and went on readjusting the balances as I played until finally I did not feel the bow at all. When I had finished it was pointed out to me in the midst of general hilarity that in my haste to illustrate the answer to a question, I had picked up a 'cello bow without realizing it.

But the most important result of the 'no bow' is that these interrelated balances also eliminate the juddering bow arm from which so many violinists suffer[8].

The legend of the violin and violin makers is well known in the musical world. The relationship between a violinist and his violin is almost unique. Most players are completely absorbed with and committed to their instrument. They are literally in love with it. The magic and mystery of the violin is based on the fact that *it is alive*. Even the naming of its different parts relates to the human body, i.e., the back, the belly and the neck. I once saw a child of six wrap up the violin in a woollen scarf as she put it in its case, with the end of the scroll peeping out like a snorkel, 'so it can breathe', she said.

But because of the three major causes of tensions discussed above, a violinist may love his instrument with all his heart, while in many cases his hand is actually strangling its neck.

As he cannot help but identify with the instrument, the cruelty of his hand (of which he is often not even aware) relates straight back to himself. Therefore it is important to realize that the hand actually needs to be trained to be tender. In my experience, the best way to do this is to keep the violin on your lap while reading, talking, or watching television. Stroke its neck with your hand (as if it were a soft, furry kitten) with the palm underneath the neck, and the fingers and thumb gently flexed inward over the strings, *but not on the fingerboard*. Pay special attention to the feeling of the thumb and make sure that it is completely fluid and mobile. For in most cases the thumb has been programmed to exert (often without the player's conscious knowledge) tremendous pressure clamped against the neck, to counteract the downward pressure of the head, bow and fingers, on the violin.

Yet the importance of a flexible, mobile thumb, and its role in musical communication, cannot be emphasized strongly enough. For example, according to scientific experiments, it seems that the thumb, with the lips and tongue, is directly connected to a special part of the brain where the motor sensory areas are located. In fact it seems that we are the only species in the world with this particular and unique construction of the thumbs. According to some anthropologists, dolphins, in spite of their intellectual capacity, cannot talk because they have no thumbs.

With the elimination of the violin hold and bow hold as we understand them, with all their vertical implications, the next important step is to eliminate the vertical action on the fingerboard. *Only then can the release of the thumb be ensured.* The best way to achieve this is to *allow* (not force!) the left wrist to fall into its natural position with the palm facing upwards. This in turn will allow a lateral slantwise action of the fingers motivated from their base joints *below the neck*. This in turn will eliminate the last vestige of vertical threat to the left thumb.

'The Havas position of the left hand is astonishingly similar in its biological foundation, if not in detail, to the unorthodox method used by Ole Bull . . . in this position the thumb acts as a movable rest for the violin, while the fingers are left absolutely free . . . what the thumb does also determines whether the hand, wrist, elbow and shoulder will be allowed to operate as one magnificent integrated system of levers, adjusting without strain to the demands of the music'.[9]

Once the integrated system in the left hand, through the fundamental balances, is established, it ensures that the so-called left hand technique, the shifts, double stops, trill, etc., become effortless musical expressions.

But the most satisfying and exciting result is in the change of tone production. The sweetness and warmth, the purity and aliveness of the tone when the tensions are released, is almost as if one could hear the violin say 'thank you' for allowing it to sing. The effect on both the player and the listener is electrifying. Of course this also applies to the viola and 'cello. As the cellist, Professor Ehrlich of Drake University, Iowa, who has adapted the New Approach to his playing and teaching, wrote in a recent letter: 'It'is marvellous when you can change a sound or face or attitude in front of witnesses and have them smile at the results.'[10]

The most interesting phenomenon was the tone produced by a deaf girl, who was trained in the New Approach in the North of England by the cellist Ian Bewley.[11] She could lip-read but could not hear at all. Yet she played the 'cello and (at my workshop) the violin, beautifully in tune, with a warm, haunting sound. When I asked her why she was playing when she was deaf, what pleasure she got out of it and how did she know when she was in tune, she made me put my hand under the back of the violin, touching it lightly while she played. It was incredible how strong the vibrations felt to the hand when she played freely without pressure, and how dead and motionless the wood felt, apart from the sound being slightly out of tune, when pressure was exerted. An even more interesting fact was that when someone played with tension and pressure producing a harsh sound, she had to leave the room because it hurt her ears.[12]

The causes for tension and anxiety in performance owing to social pressures, which prevent musical communication are manifold.[13] But two major causes apply to practically everybody. One is the desire to be loved, and the other is the fear of not being good enough.

However, when the physical tensions and mental

anxieties are released, the resulting freedom in mind and body ensures effortless musical communication as well. The performer becomes so absorbed in an organized 'inside-outward' transmission of his musical impulses that he literally has no time for doubt.

But it must be emphasized that while the gypsy can realize the power of musical communication by instinct, most traditional violinists have first to learn *how* it is possible to find this ease, and then learn how to maintain it. *The ease is there for us all to find.* It is not a question of being loose or relaxed. These are enervating, harmful concepts and conflict with the idea of dynamic power, the mainspring of musical communication. We all have this power within us and when the physical tensions and mental anxieties are released, through self-propelled unified actions, this power is transmitted to the audience.[14] This transference of energy is what effortless ease and a feeling of well-being are all about, bringing with it the most marvellous feeling of power in the world — musical communication.

All the books listed below (published by Bosworth & Co., London and Alexander Bronde Inc., New York) are by the author, except where otherwise stated.

[1] See *The Violine and I* (p. 18)

[2] See *Stage Fright*, (pp. 19, 20)

[3] See *Stage Fright*, ('The art of practicing' p. 120)

[4] See *A New Approach to Violin Playing* (p. 15)

[5] See *Stage Fright*, (pp. 18, 19)

[6] See *The Twelve Lesson Course*, (p. 4)

[7] See *A New Approach to Violin Playing*, (pp. 24, 25)

[8] For specific exercises see *A New Approach to Violine Playing*, (pp. 12-15), *The Twelve Lesson Course*, (pp. 10-26), and *Stage Fright*, (pp. 28, 38)

[9] Dr. F.A. Hellebrandt, (The Strad, 1968). For specific exercises see *A New Approach to Violin Playing*, (pp. 9, 10, 26-47), *The Twelve Lesson Course*, (pp. 27-67), and *Stage Fright*, (pp. 39-67)

[10] See *A Cellist's Guide to the New Approach,* by Claude Kenneson (Exposition Press, N.Y.)

[11] See the series, *The New Approach for Cellists,* by Ian Bewley (The Strad, 1975)

[12] See Joy Chalsworth, *Music in Ullswater* (The Strad, 1974)

[13] See *Stage Fright* ('The Social Aspect', pp. 103-117)

[14] See Dr. Ake Lundeberg, *Don't Push the River — It Flows by Itself:* Some Psychotherapeutical aspects of the New Approach (The Strad, 1976)

VILEM TAUSKY

The Conductor

Tension is a quality to be found in many situations in life and it can only be felt by those who are involved in those situations or by those who are witnessing them. Who has not witnessed the tension mount between a mother and her child until the mother slaps him and the child screams? One need only drive alongside a business man hurrying to his appointment and as the traffic lights hold him up, he will look at his watch and beat on the steering wheel with his spare hand to ease the tension. Another example is that of an audience awaiting the appearance of a great artist, when the lights are lowered, the chattering stops and one feels the tension of expectancy. Again, imagine the silence of an audience of several thousand people in a great concert hall, listening intently to the softest pianissimo of the strings. Here is another form of tension. What creates these tensions? In the first case, impatience, in the second frustration, in the third anticipation and lastly, attention.

We think of tension as a kind of invisible resilient force which pulls between a situation and a person, or, in the performance of music, between the performer and the audience. Two factors build the tensions felt by an audience: the composer and the performer.

The composer has crystalised his musical thoughts in writing the work, giving directions as to dynamics, phrasing, and tempi. He builds up tension within the

score and it is up to the performer to try to understand
the composer's ideas and convey them to the audience,
with the same intensity.

If the performer happens to be an orchestral or an
operatic conductor his responsibilities are manifold,
and so are the problems confronting him, particularly
as regards the degree and the different kinds of resulting
tensions.

In the first instance, his greatest responsibility is to
interpret the work by translating its meaning to the
audience in such a way as to convey all its subtleties,
even though the composer might not always give
clear directions.

Secondly, his instrument is a living body of musicians,
each one an individual and this naturally poses problems
of communication. The conductor is for the most part
a workman whose tools are orchestral players or singers
and he must school and control them in such a way
that every man knows precisely what to do and when
to do it.

The conductor is faced with many difficulties in
having to cope with a great number of musicians,
therefore we will study his work in the two different
situations: a) during rehearsals, and b) in performance.

Last, but not least, the conductor must have a sound
technique, as the orchestral players, and particularly
operatic singers, need a clear beat and exact indications
of his intentions.

1. Tensions within the score

There are innumerable examples of various kinds of
tensions within the score with which a conductor
is confronted.

The beginning of Beethoven's Fifth Symphony is a
case in point. It is obvious that Beethoven intends to
start building tension in the first five bars. No explicit
directions are given and musicians have interpreted it

sometimes with a slow, doomlike sound, or at other times as a fast, challenging sound. The conductor should feel free to create his own tensions which will largely depend on his reading of the rest of the score.

Two perfect examples of tension in opera arise in the Fourth Act of Puccini's *La Boheme*; one is *musical* and the other *dramatic*. The first occurs at Musetta's entrance. The students have been fooling around with fire-pokers in a mock duel, when the accompanying rumbustious music changes suddenly, with one short fortissimo chord, in a different key. The tension alters to one of tragedy which is poignantly realized by the composer.

The other depends upon the conductor and his rapport with the singers. It occurs at the end of the opera when Mimi dies. One bass note holds the tension, glances and words pass between the friends, until, at last, Rudolphe realizes what has happened. Crushing brass chords relieve the former tension, at the same time expressing his overwhelming grief.

This kind of dramatic tension can only be realized through the conductor's skill and perfect timing as well as a close collaboration with the singers.

Here intervenes the question of the role of the conductor and the need for his presence. I am often asked: "What does the conductor do? Is his presence really necessary? The players never seem to look at him."

Of course, if the conductor's work were solely to beat out time or to help keep the players together, his job would be of minor importance, though still necessary. But, he has a very different function. He has first to consider the score, decide on the shape and value of the symphony or opera, then form a realization of how the composer has gained his effects, and lastly to help the orchestra interpret them to the audience.

2. Tensions within the orchestra

a) During Rehearsals

One of the most important factors in producing a satisfying performance is the work done in rehearsals. Here tension is vital — though of a different nature than in performance — and it consists mainly in holding the interest of the players while the conductor "strips the piece down". The tension in rehearsal cannot and should not be as strong as in performance, and the time spent in "clearing up" must be fairly allotted. A too intense attitude on the conductor's part may steal some of the energy needed in the performance. As a leader once said: "You can have it now, or you can have it tonight, but you can't have both."

Let us look at the functions of the conductor at rehearsals, and then examine what means he takes to carry them out.

It is the conductor's responsibility that the orchestra should play the correct notes and, to ensure this, he must first play the work through, using his ears and eyes to check the accuracy of the music. Next, using his artistic intuition, he conveys to the orchestra the ideas he has formed about the shape and balance of the work and the relation between the various sections. He must also consider the balance of wind instruments, as each instrument in this family has a different colour and must be balanced one against the other into one chord. In some particular cases the conductor has to decide on a common breathing to achieve the desired effect. (i.e. the opening chords of the overture to Mendelssohn's *Midsummer Night's Dream*, or the wind chorale at the end of Tchaikovsky's *Romeo and Juliet*).

One of the most effective ways of rehearsing is to take one section at a time and play it through to give the orchestra an idea of the character of the music. The conductor then begins again and interrupts only if technical or interpretative changes are necessary. Finally, it is played in the form in which it fits into the whole work.

Tension is certainly lost and the musicians become bored if from the first note the conductor is incessantly interrupting. I personally do not believe it is necessary to explain the reasons for the effects one is trying to achieve. "Don't talk about why you do it, just do it," is my motto. This, the musicians understand and respect, perhaps because it allows them to get on with the work.

Freud once said that everything in life could be expressed in terms of 'tumescence' and 'detumescence' — swelling and diminution of swelling. In the performance of music we meet with one of the most common uses of tension in expressing the increases and decreases of tone. Yet even some of the best orchestras have to be reminded sometimes that the crescendo and diminuendo must be spaced evenly and gradually, and not played too suddenly. The difficulty is to spread them over a number of bars, otherwise the tension that the composer had in mind is lost and all that one hears is a steady mezzoforte.

An excellent example is the tremendous tension between the Third and Fourth Movement of Beethoven's Fifth Symphony or the slowly mounting tension to a great climax, which we find in the symphonies of Bruckner. In the same way, the great crescendi in the overtures and finales of Rossini's operas have to be perfectly spaced to achieve the effect he intended, and for which he was known as 'Mr. Crescendo'.

As with crescendi and diminuendi, so accellerandi and ritardandi are a trap for the conductor. An accellerando which is not properly spaced out will certainly ruin the tension towards which it is directed. Similarly, a badly calculated ritardando will kill the calming effect which follows a climax, or is the lead to a change of tempo.

Again, in rehearsals, the conductor must clearly establish the execution of accents and fortepianos, as marked by the composer. These should always correspond with the dynamics of the music, and he must carefully distinguish between accents in piano and accents in forte. As to the marking of fortepiano, this presents another difficulty for the orchestra. The conductor will never achieve the tension of a fortepiano if he allows it to be a forte and diminuendo in the same bar.

Though these are considerations of an aesthetic nature, inherent in the interpretation of music, they do present certain problems in rehearsal, depending largely on the skill and tact of the conductor to obtain the right response from the orchestral players.

While still on the subject of rehearsing we must examine the importance of *pauses, breaks* and *fermatas,* which are one of the most usual ways of creating and relaxing tensions. These are entirely left to the taste and discretion of the conductor. Of course we must differentiate between pauses indicated by the composer, such as one or two silent bars which must be kept in the tempo of the music unless otherwise stated, and those which are marked "G.P." or "Vuota" and can be held at the discretion of the conductor.

This freedom is very important and constitutes the basis of maintaining the tension, particularly in opera. These pauses are used mainly for dramatic effect and they call for a close collaboration between producer, performers and conductor, especially during rehearsals, when decisions have to be made. It is an advantage if the conductor is himself a pianist and is able to work together with the singers at rehearsals from a vocal score. In this way he will be ready to share the technical difficulties and the interpretation it suggests with the singers.

If the cast consists of experienced artists of certain

stature, the conductor has to be as flexible as possible
and allow them freedom for their own conception of
the particular role within the framework of the opera.
With less experienced singers, however, he must first
impress upon them the need for absolute accuracy,
and when this is achieved, he will help them to discover through the music, an interpretation of their
own. Thus, they will arrive at a fine performance,
which should be balanced between musical precision
and artistic freedom. A good example is the final
scene of Butterfly's death, in *Madame Butterfly* by
Puccini, which, although clearly outlined by the composer, gives freedom to the conductor and the singer
for a number of interpretations.

As to the controversial subject of fermatas, mainly
where singers are concerned, the collaboration between
the conductor and singers needs tact on the one side
and taste on the other. Every singer, naturally, wants
to show off his or her voice, and sometimes, especially
in Italian opera, the occasion to do so occurs too
often to be artistic. In the case of two high notes,
fairly close together, if each is given equal rubato value
by the singer the tension will be destroyed. The conductor's role is to use his skill and ability to communicate
his ideas and convince the singer — if he happens to lack
artistic taste — of the need to respect the composer's
directions. In fact, this can cause another kind of
tension, that of communication.

However, the conductor is not always right when
trying to impose the directions given in the score.
There are cases in Italian operas when *tradition* plays
a very important part and must be respected. Original
scores of famous and established composers, like Verdi
or Puccini, were published before the first performance.
Later on, from the experience gained from early performances, certain amendments were made which were
not always altered in the score. These amendments

have now become *tradition* and that is why an operatic conductor should be trained in an Opera House where he can learn the 'unwritten rules'. The final Love Duet in Act 1. of *Madame Butterfly,* or the duets of Alfred and Violetta, in Act 1 and Act IV of *Traviata* by Verdi, are very good examples of this oral tradition.

b) The Performance

By what means does the conductor hold the tension in performance, that tension which alone can make the music live? First, he must gain the respect of the orchestra or singers through a perfect knowledge of the score, of the thematic material and the orchestration. He must approach the music with sincerity, bearing in mind the composer's intentions and the indication he has given and never supersede them by an interpretation entirely of his own. One sometimes hears young conductors speaking of "my Berlioz, my Beethoven or my Mozart."

The conductor must think only of how to serve the composer and endeavour to arrive at a stylish interpretation which does justice to the score, promotes the enjoyment of the audience and gradually stamps his own work with integrity.

How is the conductor to achieve the tensions of an ideal performance? Inborn *musicality,* detailed *knowledge* of the score and *sound technique* seem to be the first requisites of a conductor.

Musicality is an inborn gift and is not influenced by the personality of the musician. It cannot be added to or subtracted from by human effort. However, sometimes, the personality draws too heavily upon the talent, and the composer suffers from an imbalance of sentiment. It is the role of the conductor to avoid overstressing the emotional value of a work. This fault becomes obvious through exaggerations of tempo in either direction and an over-emphasis of climaxes, thus producing an unbalanced performance. Perhaps one should follow Wagner's advice, to "experience first with the heart and then allow the brain to control the performance". This emotional experience can only be arrived at through a profound study of the score, the conductor trying to form his own conception of it and hear quite clearly in his own mind how he thinks the composer intended it should sound.

There is a fashion at present to conduct from memory. The only justification for this would be when the mastery of the score is so complete that its presence is more a hindrance than a help. The audience is there to enjoy the performance rather than to admire the prowess of the conductor. As long as conducting from memory is not undertaken in order to impress the audience, the decision must be entirely a matter of the conductor's choice. What is of primary importance is that he should have the score in his head and not his head in the score.

The building of tension is also achieved by means of rhythm and tempo; two very important factors, because, for the audience they form the basis of music. These factors are very much affected by the temperament of the conductor. Of course, he must respect the metronomic marks given by the composer, though very often these are arbitrary, and for some inexplicable reasons, not always correct. In such cases the conductor has to use his own judgement. In my view, the best metronome mark is measured by the feeling in your own heart. *No slow tempo must be so slow that the melody is not recognizable; no fast tempo so fast that the melody is no longer recognizable.*

The conductor must watch for another weakness which often occurs, especially in romantic music. In a crescendo, the orchestras tend to get fast and in a diminuendo, slower. These agogig changes of tempi should be carefully controlled, as, unless they are directed by the composer, they can spoil the overall effect by breaking the music into choppy waves. This happens quite frequently, particularly in some of Tchaikovsky's works, in spite of his most exact directions as to the slightest variations in tempi that he wanted. We only have to look at the opening of the slow movement in his Fifth Symphony to realize how scrupulously he has marked the slightest shades of any changes of tempo. In the same way, Mahler, himself a conductor who knew all the pitfalls, marked the changes in great detail, sometimes even adding: "Don't hurry — wait." or "Long pause, short pause".

In studying the role of the conductor in performance, we must differentiate between the work of an orchestral conductor, who is solely responsible for his performance, and that of an operatic conductor who is less dependent. He has to take many other factors into consideration. This is what Wagner wrote:

"Just as the right comprehension of the melos of a piece of music suggests the right tempo for it, so the right way of conducting an opera presupposes the true comprehension of the dramatic situation on the part of the conductor. As a matter of fact he must, before all things, have the stage in his eye. This will give him consistently, with due fidelity to the markings of the composer, the criterion as to whether he shall take the tempo faster or slower, how he shall modify it and where he shall expand or contract the volume of orchestral tone. He will not allow himself to draw a melody out at length when the phrasing should be free and animated; he will not beat out a fast tempo, effective as this may be from the merely musical point of view, where the dramatic development goes more slowly; nor will he elaborate orchestral nuances that drown the singers or divert people's attention from the events on the stage."

After examining the various roles of the conductor during rehearsals and in the performance, we must now study the conductor's technique, without which he would not be able to convey his ideas and intentions to the musicians who have to interpret the score for the audience.

3. Tensions and the conducting technique

Finally, we come to the study of the conducting technique, one of the most important factors in the realization of a fine performance. This is where the conductor may come under severe criticism from both the audience and the musicians he is working with.

It is not enough for a conductor to have a thorough knowledge of the score, he must give the orchestral players or singers a feeling of security by a confident conducting technique.

He needs a firm posture and there must be no bending backwards, as if he shrinks from the orchestra, but rather a slightly forward stance, showing that he is in command. The actual beat must be clear, in harmony with the dynamics: small in piano, growing in crescendo, decreasing for a diminuendo, short and sharp for accents, yet always in the style of the work. No grandiose, meaningless gestures, which only irritate the orchestra and distract the attention of the audience.

It is usually a fault with young or inexperienced conductors that they use too much of their body. The important tools of the conductor are the arms, hands and wrists, the eyes and the facial expression. The body should only be used to the extent that the position of the orchestra demands. If the conductor uses a stick it should be treated as a prolongation of the arm or wrist. It should be held lightly in the hand, so that a flexible wrist can indicate the beat, while the arm is mainly used to emphasize the dynamics of the music. Under no circumstances must the baton be held stiffly in the hand, because then the wrist is inflexible and the movement becomes clumsy and expressionless. There must be flexibility for the baton even in the palm of the hand.

Breathing is an important factor in conducting. It should be in harmony with the character of the music. Naturally, if the body is overstrained the conductor becomes breathless and it becomes difficult to relax the tension.

The conducting technique should be complemented by the personality of the conductor, which helps to convey his intentions to the orchestra. It is through his personality that he holds, at first, the complete attention of the players or singers. Then, through his eyes, his facial expression, and above all, by encouraging each player or group of players, with an air of expectancy, he will obtain their response.

As to the kind of tensions created through the actual act of conducting, these are similar to those confronting other instrumentalists or singers — and these have been studied in detail in the other essays of this book. There are several factors which have to be taken into consideration when studying the conductor's technique. He has to stand for a long time, both during rehearsal and in performance, facing the orchestral players or the singers, continuously exerting himself to give indications as to tempi and the interpretation of the works. It is very important indeed that there must be release of tension between the exertions. But, what is more important and valuable, is the fact that if the conductor has faithfully carried out the detailed study of the score, analysing the whole shape, its structure and orchestration, and if the work during rehearsals has been done, covering all the aspects discussed in this essay, he will find that in performance, the tensions which are the subject of this study would automatically establish themselves.

What is more, a conductor must work creatively all
the time, in rehearsals and in performance. He becomes
himself a creator who must add the quality of his
vision and imagination to the work, so that — forgetful
of himself — he recreates together with the orchestra
and through them, for the audience, the work as the
composer has imagined it.

ALFRED NIEMAN

The Composer and Creative Tension

There is an enchanting story of a Chinaman living in the T'ang dynasty, known as Hotei, who is celebrated as the Happy Chinaman or Laughing Buddha. He would not preach, or call himself a Zen master.

Instead, he walked from village to village with a big sack containing his few belongings and gifts of sweets, fruit or doughnuts which he would give to children who gathered around him in play. Whenever he met a Zen devotee or a monk, he would say with outstretched hand: "Give me one penny". Once, walking on a dusty road, he met another Zen master who stopped him and enquired: "What is the significance of Zen?"

Hotei immediately lifted his sack and dropped it on the ground in silent answer.

"Then", asked the other, "what is the consciousness of Zen?" Without hesitation the Happy Chinaman swung the sack across his shoulder and continued on his way.

If we could all receive enlightenment as simply as that, how much less confused and disturbed our lives would be. It is not the essence of life that changes, but rather the forces and pressures of our highly charged technological age. The test of the psyche to adaptation, far from being made easier by a 'smaller' world and material comfort, seems on the contrary to heighten our awareness of tension in the play of existence, and the sharp conflict of positive and negative enacting the play of creation.

The concert performer, the composer, and the group about to improvise, all know both consciously and unconsciously that a significant act of communication is about to take place which, in its highest sense, will transcend the ego and mirror the images and archetypes that inhabit the psyche.

The claim of music as the divine story-teller is not made by musicians, but rather by writers, poets, painters, and architects. From the time of the Greeks, music has been recognised as the ideal coming into expression power of the world within us. Music is a reflection of that form of cosmic energy which is life itself, in this function appearing and disappearing in eternally changing cycles of perception.

The observable phenomenon of physical tension is a direct result of our deep closeness to nature and our inability to adapt to the often violent effects of social, economic and cultural change. It is not a question of offering intellectual formulations of all possible truths, for truth is a dancer in love with paradox. That which seems out of reach should be a never-ending stimulation to explore an open-ended universe. If we find answers, we can be sure that similar answers have already been found from a different angle, especially in the East, which is already permeating the complacency of Western civilisation.

We began by considering our relation to functional life in terms of tension. Could we ask: what is tension? And can we transcend it?

The Oxford dictionary relates tension to the Latin word *tensionem*, and the French *têndre*, both meaning "to stretch".

Tension is in fact the opposite of compression or pressure.

In physics it means "a constrained condition of the particles of a body when subjected to forces acting in opposite directions away from each other, thus tending to draw them apart, balanced by forces of cohesion holding them together".

The psychology of fear is precisely such an imbalance between the two forces described above.

This may be illustrated by a simple experiment. An unknown piece of music, of moderate difficulty, is placed before a student not born with a gift for sight-reading. With some the attempt is charged with a considerable sense of panic.

Of course, this may be seen as a lack of technical mastery involving co-ordination. Fear is a destroyer. Under such conditions it is clear that true balancing of psychological tension becomes impossible. It is replaced by the ogre of physical tension, that psychosomatic shadow of man which so often results in an enormous, and sometimes very damaging, emotional resistance. It is not complacent or unreasonable to suggest that, given a more true and reachable balance of psychological polarity, it should be possible to see physical tension lessened almost to disappearing point. We are not gods; and opposites are there for our illumination. Man is an image maker, and he depends on the intuition to capture and interpret these images. But he also depends on the intuition to help him ask the right questions. Without them we flounder and turn to pedantry. To the creator and performer this is surely a vital issue, for time, treated shabbily by nervous action and reaction, is an enemy of form, freedom, and freshness (personality).

Broadly speaking, all that I have said so far is no more than a recognition of human experience. What one seeks above all, is some kind of revelation that will enhance our seeking, and verify our distance from an answer: a great purification process! We take up our seconds, minutes and hours, but when we look to the past we see an incredible landscape of rhythms over centuries, which have placed us where we are. Reaching out, it becomes possible to look back on past forms and see in action and interaction not only the wonderful syntax of musical communication present in the human psyche, but also our own period as another Rhythm in Time pointing to what Plato described as knowing: "only that it exists and that nothing else can ever be desired except in error."

And what of the tensions of our own personal rhythms? One of these, which I should like to call Emotional rhythm, is one of the charged direction-finding marks left in our conscious mind like rings on a tree, weaving itself around Growth Time, which is the biological process of all things. Growth is a lonely word. The human predicament can be seen also as a tense confrontation between the vested interests of the ego on one side, and creation as an instrument of pure consciousness on the other, the evidence of grace reflected in creativity. Art, from the village upwards, affirms a unity of life (the earth) and society. Man's spiritual problem is always the same; how to remain alive; not to be passive or dead, but to face the constant spiritual crisis.

Our world is a strange place of beauty and darkness, with so much unknown; a brief urgent existence in a brief civilisation overshadowed by a frightening forest called Nature, peered at by a few brave scientists and visionaries.

Who is to guide us? Who is to tell us that the doors we are opening are real doors to a wider vision, and not trap-doors? That our actions are not followed automatically by stumblings and disaster?

As a composer, I can try to speak effectively not only of my own awareness of the landscape in winter, my bewilderment, confusion, and ignorance, but also the exhilaration of discovery.

The tensions and problems of our time do not alter

the fact that we are living in a wonderful age. There has never been such a time as the present unless it was the astonishingly rich period of the seventeenth century, with its sense, so similar to our own, of having each foot in a different world.

It is far more hopeful too, when compassion becomes the just privilege of governments to care for those who need it.

This is the age of space. It alters and impinges upon every cobwebbed concept that stood for the moral and intellectual certitude of the nineteenth century. Our advantage is a greater honesty, more naturalness, and cleaner carpets underneath!

No tradition is healthy which lives in the past and disregards the present. Learning is a part of tradition. I have often tried to find out what 'learning' is, and I have come to the dismal conclusion that 'learning', in the sense that older generations understood it, does not exist at all. Its real form is in 'discovering', as the therapy of living is in using your self or selves. Socrates summed it up beautifully by saying: "There is no such thing as learning, one only remembers once again." Joseph Pieper (*Leisure, the basis of Culture*) aptly refers to this and says: "The teacher only induces the learner to remember and to win knowledge out of himself."

If this is the position, a higher awareness is reached between the two poles of knowledge, the physical and sensuous, and contemplation, which Heraclitus described as "Listening to the essence of things". In this creative sense, the 'doing' and the inner world of 'knowing' are both non-intellectual acts. So music, because of its abstract nature, can contact this 'remembering' more vividly than anything else.

The message of the good modern composer wears a form and content not as hedonistic indulgence, but as necessary struggle for the moment's revelation of music's spiritual speech. The challenge of throwing overboard the melody, harmony and conventional rhythm of the nineteenth century, is simply that of the son overthrowing the father's magical powers in order to find his own. The search is for identity, the content identity of now and tomorrow, at its best no less beautiful, no less affecting than the music of the past, and in one sense far more colourful. Unless we can experience knowledge as a dynamic sense of discovery, it can have very little relationship with the intuition. How then can one bring the cathartic element of teaching into play so that the tension of being can approach natural contradictions and allow them to be seen in perspective?

One way comes as a fresh wind to blow away the idea that teaching is connected only with museums. Many painters and musicians enter museums and never come out again. The past holds a magnetic attraction as an illusory source of emotional security. A museum should be a place to enter, observe, reflect and then leave for life outside.

Mahler once remarked that: "Tradition is an excuse for laziness" . . . . but it is worse than that, for in the museum mentality it is, alas, a disease transmitted to children before they can resist.

Music works at all levels; those of the ego, the super-ego, and the id. The whole range of experience opens because it manifests as communication at all these levels.

As spiritual speech it is the supreme hidden persuader. As Verlaine put it: "De la musique avant toute chose – et tout le reste est littèrature." Schopenhauer is also emphatic about the abstract nature of music: "Music is independent of the physical world . . . . and could exist, in a sense, even if there was no world . . . . . . Music is a reflection of the Will itself . . . . . . "

To reach out simply and objectively towards this

inner content requires some definition which may help us to contain these crystallised images within our limited powers of language. Leaving aside music's profound significance as a mirror of our own inner being, of both the unconscious and the spirit, it is outwardly an objective world of primal experiences: of higher tensions, and of the release of these tensions. Whether in rhythm, melody, harmony or texture, all these things can be clearly found wherever we look or listen.

Even at this stage of the twentieth century many people decipher wrongly because they are looking for the wrong thing. One has only to know where to look for the meaning — then to create, or recreate. Valid meaning rings the bell of authenticity when we respond to it as current communication. The language of James Joyce sooner or later becomes apparent for what it is — a language dealing with simple fundamental things.

The music of the nineteenth century was harmonic and romantic. The music of the twentieth is utterly different. This is a time of tremendous change when every day seems to bring something new, pushing us out further into space and consciousness. The new music reflects this energy pattern in its sprung, taut, non-pulse rhythms, spacious lines, and wide-textured harmonic palette and sound world.

With many of these thoughts in mind I began a Course of Musical Improvisation, at a University of London extra-mural class. At that time — around 1955 — I was very much a loner. Old ways die hard, and nothing of this approach was as yet being explored in education, music colleges, theatre, or cinema, and, only the first experiments of John Cage were emerging. I am referring to improvisation in a modern style, exploring new textures, sounds, and forms in the medium of chamber music with any instruments we could lay our hands on. I was very diffident about my first experiments, having little experience and even less expectation of results. What happened was staggering. The first problems were indeed involved with psychological tension, to overcome self-consciousness, shyness, violent repression, the junk of out-worn cliches, the actual fear and sense of exposure.

Gradually an atmosphere was built up — sympathetic yet demanding. Some astonishing performances took place and the personalities suddenly revealed a new light and warmth; a sense of enrichment arose, rewarding and revealing to all those involved — not least myself. Nothing deterred us. Every session I left marvelling, and thrilled by what had been created. We knew only that we had seen into each other, creating ties between us all.

It was only after the second year that I thought of taping these performances. In no sense was I fundamentally concerned at the time with the therapy of musical improvisation, and its special quality of revealing the "I" inhabiting the body. My main idea was to prove that people are capable of manifesting hidden powers in the right conditions or atmosphere and revealing them creatively and spontaneously in terms of artistic validity as form and content, as direct communication of the nowness of now. There is not space in this essay to go into an analysis of the techniques used and the many interesting and often entertaining stories and events that arose inevitably from these unconventional classes.

Speaking as one with Jungian sympathies, I discovered that reaching into people and unlocking their potentialities, involved me more deeply than my own intuition could fathom.

Through the inspiration of Jung, the practical approach of thinkers like Ouspensky and Gurdieff, and the illuminating ideas of William James (*The Varities of Religious Experience*), I began to see that in the beginning was the psyche. The psyche creates reality every day and night.

Improvisation is a way of achieving identity. The fantasy life lives in the psyche, and is manifested by deep intuitions and a quite different awareness of Time and Reality. It is an inner world of perception which, as it is seen most clearly in the small child, acts first in play and then forms concepts upon the experience, unlike the adult who is taught concepts and then attempts to pass on experiences without having known them.

The archetypes of the collective unconscious, 'the Little People', as Jung called them, are forever expressing their clashes or sympathies with the Shadow (the Fantasy Life) in our dreams. Today Dr. Hildemarie Streich, a qualified musician and psychiatrist in Germany, is opening up new fields in musical dreams. The creative aspect of the Fantasy Life has a different existence from the unconscious mind. Dr. Streich makes a reference to this in her fascinating paper "Musical motifs in Dreams". "Those dreams, in which melodies, or also melodies with text appear, which are quite original and are new creations of the unconscious are rarer than those with known musical melodies. They show us, most often, that there exist productive forces that have been, up until then, practically unused."

In seeking for a bridge between these creative forces and the conscious experience, I came to realise rather slowly and confusedly, with only intermittent flashes of light, the amazing, mysterious and 'co-rational' nature of what I call 'psychic rhythm'. I use this term to separate it from the pattern physically experienced round a pulse or beat. In our minds — above a sea of mist — we associate rhythm with the archetypal experience of physical movement, whether ritual, functional activity, or simply self-preservation.

Rhythm in this sense is a part of all of us, however

latent or repressed. Every composer knows that rhythm gives birth to his ideas; it is the father and mother of his notes.

But what gradually began to emerge in my mind was the suspected presence of a rhythmic activity that seemed to be a kind of imaginative resonator, existing beyond the boundary of purely physical (bodily) impulse.

The contact between the nervous system and the Fantasy Life might suggest that this is only a physical 'trip' — a diversionary trick. It seems to me that the problem here is not only my problem — that of words — but it is our lack of knowledge about the nature of many forms of energy, even those that are known.

The harmony of movement within the small forms (the atoms) does not make inviolate the mystery of interaction between opposites. The universe is all vibration which being energy must be sound, however immeasurable. Dr. Fritjof Capra, in his brilliant book *The Tao of Physics* (p. 158), says: "The reality of the Eastern mystic transcends the narrow framework of opposite concepts. Oppenheimer's words thus seem to echo the words of the Upanishads."

> "It moves. It moves not.
> It is far, and it is near.
> It is within all this,
> And it is outside of all this."

R. Oppenheimer: *Science and the Common Understanding*, pp. 2-3. (OUP).

The atmosphere around us is full of vibrating sounds that can be picked up by radio and radar. We too are instruments and possibly able to pick up energy influences we know nothing of. Whatever this kind of rhythm is that I am trying to convey (the problem of the unpredictability of some particles is a physicist's problem, not mine!) its action on human beings in a still state is creative in that it stimulates, and can knife its way through even inert thought once an instinctual contact with it is made. Constant encouragement to my improvising students to let go the deeply rooted habits of nursery and platitudinous rhythms and discover their own innate images, often resulted in astonishing flights, bold outbursts of shape and form.

I do not think this can be explained by nervous physical energy alone, but rather by this hidden persuader. This strange source "psychic rhythm" is potentially there, ready to act upon us — not as a current of electricity or the brain setting up conditioned wave reflexes — but as a *conscious* energy (if there is such a thing) might do if it landed on a responsive psychic field, which *then* could act also on the physical body.

This may well seem nonsense but my experiences have provoked me to look for something beyond the seemingly natural world of musical rhythm. I suggest that this co-ordinated play of tensions would be a worthwhile field for scientific exploration. If it can act on musical invention, then it should be able to act on whatever medium is willing to accept it, including other forms of creativity unconnected with music. Rosamond Lehmann, the novelist, supported this theory in describing the way her own characters came to life before she started to write. In the recent conference of internationally famous scientists at Lake Como, organised by Arthur Koestler and chaired by the late Professor Waddington of Edinburgh University, the aim was to find new explanations for the origins of life. The question of new rhythms in Time came up, with much significance, in conflict with the idea of continuity and some aspects of Darwinian theory.

One development in my work with improvisation was that I became drawn into the brave new and revolutionary world of Music Therapy. To train students to

use these improvising skills with mentally and physically
handicapped children is also to help the students to
know themselves. The therapist must build a bridge
to communicate with these children who, because of
their disabilities, live in a painful world of isolation.

Many of these children cannot speak, but the child's
singing voice can and does respond to the vocal and
pianistic improvisation of the therapist. A drum and
cymbal can stimulate a child to share in the experience
of the mood, and from there enter into a meaningful
activity whose cathartic effect penetrates the child's
personality. This can apply to individual and group
sessions. The power of music to evoke this intercom-
munication leads to a working relationship which has
already shown its power to have far-reaching consequences, bringing a sense of meaning and order to the
mentally or emotionally disabled. Thus the ancient
practice of music healing is brought to a scientific
level in studies leading to research and more discovery.

If sickness creates isolation, then music communicated
and shared in improvisation can be the stretched-out
hand that restores hope and the meeting of eyes. We are
all asking how we can escape from the savagery of
mental oppression into spiritual freedom; from the
sickness of violent tension into lyric release. This is
where improvisation has shown its power to act.

I must, however, stress that improvisation is not just
a function of therapy, important thought that is, but a
means of valid artistic creation. To normal people that
is its aim, its purpose, its significance. To discover and
reveal the innate artistic power of the human soul to
individualize musical language into a personal expression
— power, to free the means of communication between
the Fantasy Life and the conscious being: the bridge of
meaning in life. Thus after each performance we criti-
cise and comment on the level of achievement quite

frankly and freely, knowing that the listener's response reveals the listener equally to himself and others. Its invaluable use in education in schools is again to release high energy tension and to prove to normal children that music is something from inside coming out, not merely something from outside going in. For many composers too (one thinks of Stravinsky) it is the raw material for their strictly disciplined work. It is a method of release from the repressions and tensions of the world of conformity, yet its value and beauty lie in active participation, the sharing of experience. The listener who feels the creative force is not without reward either, vicarious though it may seem, for it is the open door to the Self. Its immortality is in its power to stimulate, to evoke, AT THE MOMENT.

So we come full circle to the composer carrying his creative cross on his back. The tensions he offers us are our own tensions, the crystallised images in melody and rhythm our own images, both of the soul and dipped in the deep unconscious, revealing the primeval sources from which we all spring, and reminding us of our deepest knowledge, the sounds of all nature, our fears and our play, and our love. Through the duality of tension we are given a wonderful peep into the blessing of being born in the human body. The anima is ever present to lead us into higher levels of inner perception before we can take 'a mortal leap' as Henri Bergson described it, to the Truth.

So far I have only generalized about my own experiences, which have been generated by music. Is it possible to justify these theories with an equation that fits the need of both psychologist and logician? Identity is the knowledge of the Self. These people communicating to each other were discovering their own rhythm.

But what is music?

A little boy of five wrote a poem:

"An apple you eat
A bee that stings
A castle with towers
A lemon that sings."

If you are charmed by something in this imaginative
vision, you cannot put it down merely to the rhyme.

Nor is music just order, or organisation of sound.
It consists of a resonator which echoes from our inner
reality into physical manifestation. This is content in
music. It consists of unconscious images. They are not
the same thing as musical form. These images are
crystallised by the composer into shapes (melodies
or rhythmic figures having some kind of textural or
harmonic implication).

This is how they are received by the listener — as
musical ideas in time. In the process, the unconscious
mind of the listener acts as a catalyst and returns the
music to its original symbolic nature, its archetypal
image.

A composer casts his music in a form, a mould,
which is immensely important to him as any architect
would recognise, for it is his special approach to that
which one can be consciously aware of; the outer
structure, the main design, the look of it, as it were.

This is only the tip of the iceberg. The essence of the
content is enormous and unbelievable in its effect. The
more the composer enters into the stillness, which is
the perfect balance between the tensions of the spirit
and the unconscious, the more will these images and
their constant re-creation be present.

Thus with composers like Monteverdi, Mozart,
Beethoven, Bach, Schubert, Stravinsky, Stockhausen,
to name but a few, the images are buried deep below
the surface. Debussy understood this very well when
he wrote in a letter to Stravinsky (about the "Rite
of Spring"): "There is in it a kind of sounding magic,

a mysterious transformation of mechanical into human souls, by a spell whose invention seems to me to belong only to you. . . . "

This is interesting because in Debussy's own later impressionistic music, the content is practically on the surface by reason of the very nature of its impressionistic purpose. Even so, Debussy achieves many strokes of genius in his resilient image-world.

The masculine and feminine in the form of the anima spin their play of creation in human nature. Perhaps the last word could go to Dr. Fritjof Capra who included in his *The Tao of Physics* (Wildwood House, London, pp. 259) a photograph of colliding particles in a bubble-chamber combined with a drawing of the dance of Shiva and then commented:

"For the modern physicists then, Shiva's dance is the dance of subatomic matter. As in Hindu mythology, it is a continual dance of creation and destruction involving the whole cosmos; the basis of all existence and of all natural phenonemena. Indian artists created visual images of dancing Shivas in a beautiful series of bronzes. In our time, physicists have used the most advanced technology to portray the patterns of the cosmic dance. The bubble-chamber photographs of interacting particles, which bear testimony to the continual rhythm of creation and destruction in the universe, are visual images of the dance of Shiva equalling those of the Indian artist in beauty and profound significance. The metaphor of the cosmic dance thus unifies ancient mythology, religious art, and modern physics. It is indeed, as Coomaraswamy has said: "Poetry, but none the less, science".

Since all vibration is also sound, the poetry is indivisible from music, and the dance from rhythm. At the heart of the Universe, the Music of the Spheres identifies itself with eternal creation. The essence of music is "I am".

WALTHER GRUNER

Voice Production and Body Co-ordination

(To the memory of Hermann Grünebaum)

Genesis (II) ". . . and there, confound their language, that they may not understand one another's speech." The people of Babel, to whom this refers, seem to have been teachers of singing as they, most certainly, have no common language. The laryngologists have, but there is a wide gap in communication between the empirical experience of the singing profession and the medical men.

What has all this to do with tensions and relaxations? If we cannot decide what produces a good singer we are also at a loss about remedies, should they be necessary.

I would therefore like to begin at the end, with two examples of vocal perfections that immediately spring to my mind.

At the age of about twenty, when I was studying singing and highly interested in voice production, I heard Battistini. He was seventy at the time of his concert in Leipzig, and the sensational and unforgettable finding was that his way of singing was on a completely different level from anyone I had heard. Here was the perfect Bel Canto singer. All the notes produced were of a pure resonance without any extraneous noises. His agility was like that of a coloratura soprano. The uninterrupted easy flow of his voice never made me, as a listener, anticipate any difficulty as is so often the case with even well-known professional singers

This unforgettable experience was so startling that I discussed it with my teacher and remember saying: "If the method of this singer is right, then all, and I mean all other singers I have heard so far in my life (and I come from a family of musicians and singers) are nothing more than beginners as far as voice production is concerned."

The second overwhelming impression took place around 1935, at Covent Garden. I had a good seat in the stalls for a performance of *Die Walküre* and the singer, Kirsten Flagstad (then unknown to me) came down from the mountains (in Act II) and sang the famous "Hojoteho". The sensation of this vocal outburst is as unforgettable as the artistry of the Bel Canto mentioned earlier. I should like to explain why I specifically referred to the seat in the stalls. My immediate reaction to her call to nature was to look up and around me as I could not believe that this wonderfully clear, round sound came from the back of the stage. I looked round again, and even up to the ceiling of the Opera House. I was surrounded by sound from all sides. One never had the impression that the voice was 'produced' nor was there any sign of diaphragmatic energy transmitted to me as a listener.

A vocally aware listener is so sensitive to a singer's vocal sensations that he almost experiences them — just as when someone yawns we are inclined to do likewise — and a teacher of Voice Production should be particularly receptive in this respect. Also, a good singer's seemingly effortless flow of tone has a most beneficial effect upon his listeners, just as strained and inhibited singing can often have a bad effect, not only on the listeners but also on other participants in an ensemble.

This effortless flow of tone in fine singing could be compared with the performance of a car of quality, like a Rolls-Royce, which *glides* along noiselessly,

while all inferior cars *work* and the engine wears out. . .
and so does the singer who uneconomically burns up
his energy.

In this context, Ljuba Welitsch comes to mind,
she certainly was the best imaginable Salome, but the
high tension in her singing made me wonder whether
her voice would last another few years. The question
arises whether such an outstanding artist would have
accepted the advice to practise some relaxation exercises, Yoga or Alexander Technique . . .

At this point, I am also thinking of Maria Callas,
most likely the most musical of all these artists and,
in her earlier days, with almost unlimited vocal ability
— as one can hear from her early recordings. A 'high
tension vibrato' was noticeable, but as long as the voice
was used with flexibility (as in *I Puritani*) no harm could
have been done. But, then, Bel Canto singing could
not fulfil her dramatic personality, so she had to sing
Tosca. Yet already her Tosca was dominated by her
intellectual vision of *Music Theatre* and, this forced
her to move away from Puccini's conception of the
part, and we were offered, instead, an almost irresis-
tible Greek revolutionary woman. Callas herself mentioned (in one of her highly intelligent television inter-
views) that she did not like singing 'Vissi d'arte', as,
from her point of view, it only held up the action.

This 'Music Theatre' conception made her force her
alto vocal chord function upwards and this was bound
to lead to an early decline of her voice. (Pop-singers
may do this, for a while, though, only with the help
of microphone amplification).

I began this article with the end result. Now I would
like to go to the very beginning. The newly born baby
greets the world with an anxiously awaited cry. The first
breath goes together with the first cry. From then
onwards, that baby cries on and off and the little body,
often weighing not more than 6 or 8 pounds, produces

unbelievably penetrating noises — quite out of proportion to anything an adult can consciously produce. Inhibitions or tensions do not exist.

At a later stage, at the age of about three or four, all these former babies take to singing. Whatever they want, they will express in a calypso-like style of singing. "Mummy, can I have my cocoa?" is now communicated in song form. When the child goes to school *this direct vocal improvisation* disappears, and only a small percentage of children retain what we usually call a *singing instinct*.

There are children who are born singers — they will most likely *speak uninhibitedly* from the diaphragm — and there are others who are being told over and over again to keep quiet, not to be so noisy, and are being conditioned to think that soft speech is refined. Occasionally there is an unhappy child who has been told that he has an ugly voice — and this is a major crime. This will most likely be enough to prevent him from ever becoming a singer. The retention of an uninhibited outlet in vocal form is the basis of what we call a born singer.

There is a distinct difference between the age when a student of singing can start to train the voice and that of a student of an instrument. A child of six or seven can start to learn the piano or a string instrument and continue uninterruptedly until he can pursue it professionally. It is not the same with a singer who can only be trained when he is sexually mature and the vocal cords have reached their ultimate strength and size. A *singer's instrument* does not consist only of *vocal cords* and *vocal box,* but *his whole body* is involved. The *voice has to be 'produced',* and obviously this is easier to achieve with a 'born singer'.

It is often quite wrong to regard the singing and the voice of the young untrained student as unspoilt since the Art of Singing demands that the voice should be 'produced'. (In fact, the author of this essay insists on calling himself a teacher of Voice Production and not a Singing Teacher.)

In training students of singing, one must make a distinction between *natural musicality* and *academic musicianship*. The *singing instinct* of the child is at the root of natural musicality while academic training and musicianship will lead to *consciousness and control*. It may sound rather commonplace to state that only a combination of these two qualities makes a good singer and musician.

As far as potential singers are concerned, the retention of the singing and play instinct is a most important factor. The process of *falling into awareness* will often suppress this instinct and one of the tasks of the teacher, when dealing with the grown up beginner, is to *retrace and unravel* that delightful childhood directness. No wonder, then, that singers of Opera are of a happy and relaxed disposition, as most of them have retained that instinct and, through singing and acting, tensions and inhibitions are superbly dealt with.

Training singers is a great responsibility for a consciencious teacher. The student must be fully grown, and certainly, a combination of the singing instinct (recognisable from his or her phrasing) together with a basis of academic musicianship, is a prerequisite. It is very rare indeed that a youngster, between approximately sixteen or twenty years of age, would immediately convince his future teacher, at the first audition, that he will make the grade. Even after examining the voice *beyond* listening to one or two songs or arias, he will still need three months, or sometimes longer, before reaching a responsible conclusion as to how far an ambitious student will go. There are physical and mental restrictions and inhibitions to be watched and treated and the natural relationship between these is very complex. A typical example is Richard Tauber who had no voice and conductors and producers tried to dissuade him from his singing ambitions. But he *had* to sing and luckily found the right teacher.

Breathing in ordinary life is subconscious and automatic. Breathing in singing is fundamentally different. The breath has to be arrested, and this means that the inhaling period is very short and the exhaling consists in prolongued control. The right relationship between *poised breath* and *relaxation* is one of the main features of voice production. In many ways the problems are similar to sports training. A good singer will have learnt to 'support' his voice *without involving other parts of the body which should remain in a state of relaxation.*

When a pianist wishes to play a serene or happy piece of Mozart he will never frown and if he plays the first chords of Beethoven's 'Pathétique' Sonata he will find it impossible to smile at the same time.

When a singer sings a passage which causes him difficulties, *facial tension*, and in particular, *frowning* will be evident. If this singer sings the same passage in front of a mirror (and of course has no other musical worries at that moment) and *forces* himself not to frown, he will be surprised to find that this alone will 'unforce' the strain and the dreaded fear of that musical passage will disappear.

There is a kind of person who has a habit of wearing a monocle. (I think, and I hope, that species is on the decline!) The monocle-wearer who jams a glass into his eye usually explains this by stating that he is short-sighted in one eye only. This, at best, is self-deception. It actually is the expression of a specific attitude towards his fellow men. A monocle wearer is a person who wants to assert his authority. And, in such a person, *uninhibited natural emotion cannot find uninhibited outlet,* as indeed, this self restraint is imposed by this very attitude. Natural laughter has become impossible, while the facial tension of our monocle-wearer influences his coordination, resulting in body stiffness and rigidity.

I gave two examples of tension: 1. the expression of anxiety and 2. a self willed rigidity. These demonstrate the inter-relation between mind and body. The separation of physiology and psychology is basically wrong and I chose these particular examples of facial tension to illustrate this point.

If we think in terms of cause and effect, at least as far as body tension is concerned, this is rather superficial.

Body control and body relaxation will influence the mind just as much as mind control will influence body tension or relaxation. The little tension of frowning I referred to, consciously removed by looking into the mirror, can have far reaching effects, because the few little muscles seem to have sent a telegram with great speed saying "no cause for anxiety". We know so much nowadays about 'feed-back' and other physiological processes, that it is high time to realize that it is useless simply to tell a performer "do not be afraid and use *self-control* to overcome *stage fright*". It is normal to be anxious and it is normal to have stage-fright, and a one-sided psychological approach to solve these tensions is insufficient. Just as the monocle gives an exaggerated and unpleasant stiffness, which is symptomatic of the personality of the wearer, a *coordinated body control will remove tension-producing anxieties.* Here again, we have to keep in mind that the poised breath which does not involve other unnecessary tensions will give the singer self-confidence.

The expansion of the lower ribs to which the otherwise dome-shaped diaphragm is attached, will add additional air. If this diaphragmatic extension is exaggerated it leads to what we call a "stomach press", and the ensuing body rigidity must be avoided under all circumstances. The amount of *air intake* itself is only of *secondary importance.* The air control — i.e. slow and regular release — is the major factor in breath control. The controlled decrescendo is more difficult to achieve than the crescendo (more of this later on when dealing with Messa di Voce).

Breathing exercises should enable the student to arrest his breath, while standing errect. Then he must try *to swing his arms* or *his head* in rotating movements, while maintaining the balance of the body. These movements have to be executed slowly, stressing the relaxation factor. When a piano pupil starts his lessons, his teacher will, most likely, lift his fore-arm with one finger and make it clear that when he releases it, the arm should fall down and swing until it comes to rest.

The student of singing has to learn what muscular relaxation means. Just as a cyclist will go down a hill free-wheeling and will be half-way up the next hill without using energy, the singer has to experience *how little physical work is actually* necessary. The feet should be firmly positioned on the ground, slightly apart, otherwise our singer will sway like a reed. This pressure of the feet should still enable him to move his body from the knees. I do not however propagate that Oratorio or Opera singers should imitate the late Elvis Presley!

There are tensions which have to be consciously avoided — and where training is necessary — concerning the movements of the jaw. The normal jaw movements used in chewing or speaking are not sufficient for the singer. He must learn to relax the jaw, as it is only attached to the skull by muscles and if he should ever look at a skeleton, he would see that the jaw has to be attached with a piece of string. The singer should be able to unhinge (if I may use an unscientific word) the jaw, more or less like a village idiot. There is no danger that this could lead to a tremolo. On the contrary. Tremolo — except when showing symptoms of old age when there is a slackness in the vocal cords – is produced by other tensions. If a high dramatic soprano sings with a jabbering jaw, this is produced by these tensions and is often called "over-singing".

A dancer cannot work with a full stomach, as the inner section of the diaphragm *loses its elasticity*. The young singer on the platform, unable to keep his breath still will lose grip of his lower notes, as the diaphragm will push the air column too much against the vocal box. In short, he will sing as if he had eaten too much. Professional singers have a practical way of discussing these matters. They will differentiate between singing "on the breath" or "with the breath". The petrol tank of a car does not supply petrol directly to the engine, but this flows steadily into the carburetter, which in turn supplies the engine with a *minimum of petrol.*

The question of breath support requires a closer investigation. The two ideal vocalists mentioned at the beginning of this essay *sang economically*. The analogy with cars which have a big petrol tank and petrol reserve, clearly illustrate my point. In the same way, no matter how powerfully a great singer may occasionally sing, the listener always has the wonderful experience that there is still more in reserve.

The old Italian School considered "messa di voce" one of the most important elements of vocal training, and most recent research into the vocal cord action proves the 18th century Bel Cantists correct. A note is correctly produced only if it can be swelled or unswelled. When listening to Caballe or some of our coloured singers, you can hear how they start pianissimo on the highest note, releasing more air, which means crescendo, and then they do a decrescendo again. Whilst writing this article I had the pleasure of hearing Caballe on the radio singing Puccini's "In Quelle trine Morbide" and the most wonderful effect she achieved was the decrescendo after a big emotional climax. This easy flow cannot work if there are any unnecessary tensions.

I have mentioned above that the principles of Bel Canto, as we know them, are in keeping with our latest knowledge of vocal cord structure. The swelling and unswelling of a note means that the tightly closed vocal cords — which might well be called vocal lips — are activated with the minimum of air. The vocal cords will respond in the way the Old Italians took for granted, only if this edge movement is not forced by too thick an air column. Actually, some sopranos find that there is a "flute register" which can extend their range considerably (as in the case of Gracie Fields).

However, this is not the place to talk about voice production in general, as the purpose of this article is to talk about the negative side — i.e. the tensions which should be avoided, and inhibitions which should be eliminated.

We have to realize that the end of the vocal cords are attached to cartilages which are linked to the vocal box. The whole mechanism can well be compared with mobiles as they are often found particularly in children's rooms. The vocal box itself, as it is well known, is directly connected to the root of the tongue. Many singers, and this is a very understandable tendency, will press their breath (i.e. the air column) upwards when the musical line goes that way. In doing this, they often interfere with the normal position of the box. This box must remain in a low, but flexible position, otherwise the throat and in particular the width of the pharynx will be narrowed. The narrowing of the pharynx results in the production of sharp, edgy sounds. The voice is artificially narrowed, squeezed, and becomes lifeless, through the displacement of the voice box. Singing sharp is usually not caused by a lack of ear training but by aggressive production, just as flat singing is often the after effect of undue tension.

The natural and absolutely necessary *vibrato* will cease. It is futile to draw too much attention to the position of the tongue in the mouth. In every day life, when there is no intention of producing poised singing, the tongue will lie peacefully in the mouth, and the tip of the tongue will rest below the lower teeth. It should remain like this in singing. One of the dangers of throat narrowness would then be avoided. If the tongue slips back, the big section of the tongue which is ultimately attached to the vocal box, will then unduly narrow the throat, but this can be corrected by the unhinging of the jaw. When the vocal box is pushed upwards we get the effect of a dumpling in the throat. In German it is known as 'Knödel' and the expression of 'Knödeltenor' is often heard, as tenors are most likely to commit this error.

I should like to return now to the question of basic breath control. The actual *quantity of air intake is of secondary importance.* The method, however, of holding the breath is vital. The inflation of the lungs must not, under any circumstances, create *tension of the neck muscles.* Raising of the shoulders will immediately produce that effect.

As I have mentioned before, the singer's instrument is not only his vocal cords and his resonator, but ultimately, his whole body. It is quite an experience to watch Muhammed Ali in action and see the correct relation of *strength and flexibility.* This does not mean that a great boxer would make a great singer, but singers could learn a great deal from this boxer! In the same way, it is easier for the Opera singer, who sings flexible and agile music, to find the right balance, than for a concert singer. Also, concert-platform, or radio, for that matter, make high demands on the singer's body coordination, which has to be more subtle, while an experienced opera singer can get away with inferior vocalism. The audience gets involved in the visual aspect of the performance. If an operatic Buffo singer is guided by his musicality, and his movements are not superimposed, but develop out of the spirit of the music (i.e. the phrasing) his performance will be best coordinated. A splendid example of this is Geraint Evans, who himself said: 'I can only sing when I act'. He does not first act and then incidentally sing. In this respect one must learn to differentiate between the *acting singer* and *the singing actor.*

We have reached now the question of *relation between singing and speaking.* When there is no unnecessary pressure upwards (i.e. when a basic singing attitude has been established), the varying vowels and consonants can be formed with tremendous speed without any strain. This applies at least to the low and middle range of the voice. Here the Italian is certainly at an advantage, as there is not much difference between his speaking and singing. His speaking is already singing. The Welshman's speech has a sing-song melody, which also narrows the gap between speech and the 'produced' voice. This explains why there are so many 'born singers' in Naples or in Wales. In our old established universities a hesitation, even a slight stammer in speech, was (?) sometimes regarded as a symptom of modesty and cultural refinement.

Stammering and stuttering are extreme examples of diaphragmatic spasm. In singing, a person thus afflicted can overcome it, but, in my experience he will be inclined to *oversing*, and the problems which terrify him will not be solved in parlando recitativo.

The acting-singing of recitatives is of greatest importance. The combination of intelligent word treatment and musical phrasing, the projection of small values — all these are as important as singing big arias. *Flexibility first and sustained legato later!*

This brings me to the problem of the singer's musicianship. There are many occasions when academically *essential knowledge hampers the free flow of air.* How can this be? Music, as we understand it up to computer serialism, begins with two notes and their relation. In singing (i.e. voice production) we are confronted with a basic outlet, an act of *creative production.* The act of singing should be fundamentally a *joyous and physical* pleasure. This applies even to the singing and interpreting the saddest of music. Self-pity and lacrimosity is not the basic approach to singing be it the *St. Matthew Passion* or *Tristan and Isolde.*

The student of singing often has to be guided to find his true voice. Sometimes, he may be inclined to imitate a much admired artist, and this has now become quite a problem in our "recordings age". However, if only one single note is freed from intellectual interference, this can help him to gain *that joy of direct creativity.* Can one discuss this with the Neapolitan fisherman in his sun-drenched boat? The singer must not, and cannot realize this by listening to and hearing the sound he is producing, but must learn to register the sensation of an open throat and the unique pleasure when there are no obstacles, no muscular tension in the way.

May I now quote Dr. Percy Judd, author of "A Singer's Musicianship". '. . . . A Music College is a place where you cannot apply in "room 27" what you learnt in "room 48".'

Let me use two examples: first, learning how to trill, and secondly, how to sing chromatic scales. In our imagined 'room 48' — the room for musicianship lessons — the student is given "vocal exercises" and is asked to sing one whole tone up and down, first in crotchets, (quarter notes) then quavers (eighths) and semiquavers (sixteenths) and this is supposed to lead him or her to a rhythmically controlled trill. Of course it does not. Those naturally uninhibited and those we call gifted, can do it anyhow, while the vast majority will not learn it. Why? because it is "the cart before the horse".

If this vocally helpless singer turns up for his singing lessons ('room 27') I start by freeing the voice box and make our momentarily 'over-disciplined vocalist' warble, regardless of exact measure of whole tone interval and completely abandoning rhythmic discipline. I then ask the student to produce scales with gradually increasing compass (never from tonic to octave!) on a *rolling "r"*. Most likely he cannot produce this straightaway as a 'stomach press' paralyses the freedom of the tongue movement. This situation actually is similar to the moment of extreme fear when a victim cannot utter a sound until the tiger has left the room! The quick movement of the tip of the tongue cannot be achieved by exercising conscientiously and consciously the tongue alone. This, our 'militarised' academic singer-to-be, will try — since he was brought up to believe in discipline: "try, try, and try again". But when he is *shown body relaxation movements (neck and knees in particular)* this will very quickly free his vocal box, as knee movement would influence and prevent diaphragmatic spasm. Often neck rotation and circular hand movements from the wrist will achieve the freedom for quick tongue movement. In over forty years of teaching I have met only one student who had a 'thick tongue' and only one student who was *unwilling* to relax.

The next step is to ask my frustrated warbler to move his arm upwards from the elbow, so that the wrist is on a level with his neck and ask him to move the hand in quick rotation motions from the wrist. If he cannot do this and is too rigid, then the arm must first hang loosely and the hand movement executed in a hanging down position until the hand can shake freely, rotating to and fro. When the student does this hand-wrist motion and at the same time produces a note, preferably in the range between d^1 and f^1 (according to the

type of voice), he will warble. The diaphragm and the
breath will act in coordination. Diaphragm-breath action
is a slow process, in contrast to brain-vocal chord action
which works with lightning speed. When the student
has been able to 'warble' freely, then and only then can
the disciplines of 'room 48' be applied.

Before dealing with the second example, (the execution of the chromatic scale) I should like to discuss
the shortcomings of our 'room 48' disciplines. Most
exercises required for examinations, are not good for
basic voice production. The voice requires *scales in
curves* (like a roller-coaster at a fun fair), smaller circles
and then wider ones — starting on the fifth moving
down to the tonic, then from the ninth, but not yet
to the octave. The scale to the upper octave·is conditioned by harmony and the tension from the *seventh
to the octave* should be avoided at the beginning.
When you throw a stone into a pond, wider and wider
rings begin to form, and similarly, our young singer
will extend his range, *not in straight, geometrical
lines,* up and down, but in *curved vocal lines.* Only when
the singer has gained an almost complete range and has
sufficient vocal freedom to sing within that range,
— so that he can sing softly with support and crescendo
and decrescendo — the essential academic discipline
should be introduced. The prerequisite of basic training
which I have described above, will then bear fruit.

One of the main considerations is the undisputed,
but often mismanaged fact, that *thinking,* in contrast
with *experienced sensations,* must not interfere at the
wrong moment. Even a genius like Einstein could not
think of two things simultaneously. Singing requires
planning before action, but as it is *an act of creativity,*
thought must not hamper it. The coordination between
timing of breathing and thinking (planning and sound
production) is a vital issue.

To return now to the execution of the chromatic

scale. As we know it, this scale is a mechanical division of an octave into twelve equally distant semitones. My imaginary student learns how to do this in our 'room 48'. Coming to his singing lesson, he or she will do this accurately if he sings it *unsupported,* and possibly with 'la-la-la' interruptions *and minimum of voice.* The same musically sound student — a student who hears the scale in his head clearly, in pitch — will find that he is unable to sing it with full voice. Often there will be more, and some times less. He may get to the octave, but in between, accuracy of pitch and even the right amount of notes will not be produced. 'Room 48' has failed again. The bigger the vocal material, the more emotional the singer, and the greater is then the failure.

Again, through coordinated hand movement — this time not in order to relax, but *to discipline and mechanise* the proceedings — one can overcome these difficulties. The *voice* cannot be told to sing in pitch. *Pitch will regulate itself automatically by subconscious brain-vocal cord action,* which works with lightning speed. Adjustment by breath is too slow and clumsy.

I have met students with three or four years college or private training who failed to sing correctly a chromatic scale. They were quite surprised to find that within ten minutes this was solved through certain mechanical and rigid movements of the hand and one finger. This brought about the *recognition that pitch accuracy does not depend on ear training, but on controlled breath* — which is a *vital point.*

The brain vocal cord connection works with the speed of electricity. A singer must never try to find the notes with his vocal mechanism. It is advisable that the singing teacher (in "room 27") should also insist that the student *beats time or conducts whilst he sings.* This is helpful — not only for the "room 48" disciplines — but because it excludes over-emotionalism and steadies the diaphragm. It is interesting to note that the 'Dalcroze' method and 'Tonic-Solfa', using hand movements, have all been developing in the same direction.

Uninterrupted regulated flow of air rarely harms a voice, but stop/go methods are dangerous for the vocal cords. Certainly over-singing and shouting is bad, but switching on and off in the middle of a run or phrase is far worse. It is better to sing a wrong note here and there, and, likewise, wrong words or lost words are not first considerations. And petty interference — like Beckmesser — kills the singing impetus and can lead to hoarseness or other worse damage of cord action.

In my opinion, it is essential to become first a vocalist then an artist. In instrumental music two notes are the beginning of music. The singer need sing only *one note* and by this creative act can find his *true* self. Singing is a creative process and interpreting Mozart, Bach, Wagner, or Verdi will follow. The other way, the singer will never attain true self-confidence. He then will have to interpret the great music as best he can, but will not be able to put his voice freely to the service of the composer's demands. This will lead to archness, sentimentality in place of true sentiment, and ultimately a lack of integrity.

I was asked once by a professional bass to hear him in a concert and give him an unbiased opinion. He was shocked when I told him that there was only one item in which his voice sounded really beautiful — and that was the encore. The job was over, and so were all his inhibitions and tensions. The encore was not by Mozart or Verdi, but a less important song and, unexpectedly, he was able to produce a noble and beautiful sound. The reverence he had for a great aria of Sarastro, or King Philip's beautiful aria in *Don Carlos*, had away a great deal of his potential vocal beauty.

A last word on the training of a soloist. As his body is his instrument, the teaching should take place in *class-work*, in the presence of some of his colleagues. In this way, he not only gets used to an audience, but also learns a great deal while listening to his colleagues. It would be of immense value if he could have shorter lessons (of say, fifteen minutes) several times a week, being shown how to practice. Unfortunately, these 18th century conditions of studying cannot be realized today, therefore, a minimum of two forty-five minute individual lessons, plus listening-in to the work in the class, is essential.

In conclusion, I should like to sum up the main points of this essay:

Mind and body are one.

Coordinated movements should help to steady or relax the body, according to necessity.

The timing of thinking (planning) and the succeeding actions has to be continuously watched.

Closer coordination between teachers of 'Voice Production' is greatly needed, which perhaps will bring about some changes in the methods of teaching — i.e. 'room 27' or 'room 48' are often to be blamed for causing a great deal of tension.

The singer's true personality must be freed and guided.

The *source* of the vital self confidence cannot be achieved through academic learning.

And finally, Voice Production and Singing is an ART not a SCIENCE.

I would like to close with a saying of Goethe *(Tasso):*

"So fühlt man Absicht und man ist verstimmt"
("You note the intention and it spoils your enjoyment")

LEIGH HOWARD

Freeing the Voice for Actors and Opera Singers

To write about tension is to write about a subject that has many facets. Tension, it is said, is caused by stress, which in turn arises from fear — fear of inadequacy, fear of criticism, fear of the unknown. To define the resulting tension, let alone alleviate it, is much harder. Since there is now a great deal of research into the causes and relief of tension it is probable that our knowledge of how to deal with it will be greatly expanded. But the actor, singer and indeed any interpretative artist will always be faced with stressful situations by the very nature of his art and must learn how best to deal with them as they arise, and with the limited knowledge at his disposal.

In this essay we are to consider the effects of tension on the voice of the actor or the operatic singer, when he is confronted by the need to combine singing with speech in opera. Many singers treat dialogue in opera much as the Children of Israel viewed the Red Sea — the gulf between themselves and the Promised Land. This in itself breeds anxiety that creates tension, which, in turn affects the voice.

The training of opera singers and indeed singers in general, in the study of Speech and Drama, is similar to that of actors. They should be taught to develop and control the voice so that it may be fully expressive of the characters they are to play. Training should emphasise the importance of relaxation in this respect and should suggest ways in which singers and actors may learn to free themselves from tension in rehearsal, before and during performance.

It is this aspect of the work that will be discussed here.

From the beginning of his training, the actor like the singer, encounters stress in one form or another. His first presentation of himself as candidate for audition in one of the colleges may be his introduction to this stress, but from the moment his training begins, to the end of his career, he will find himself in countless situations where fear and anxiety will take possession of him. His mouth may go dry, his voice sounds harsh and strangled, his gestures become stiff and inexpressive. He will feel that the audition is going badly, that he is not doing himself justice. First nights become nightmares — will he remember his lines? Will his voice survive the evening? Will he? Even in the comparatively sheltered life of the college he is on trial, subject to competition with fellow students. He may have problems of coordination, or his voice be unmusical, fettered by an unattractive native accent. He may not at first be aware of these handicaps, and his growing realisation of how much he needs to learn — or even undo — can make every class an ordeal as he struggles with his difficulty.

Like the singer, the actor is his own instrument. His voice, his body, his inner self, must co-ordinate if he is to be fully expressive. His imagination and his understanding of the character he is to play must be reflected in a body supple and responsive to these demands. His voice must be flexible, capable of a great variety of pitch and colour, reacting instantly to the subtleties of the text and the emotional range of his part. How are these desirable qualities to be maintained under the stress of performance? How is the tension, that performance almost invariably brings, to be controlled so that the artist may realise in full all the qualities of the character he is called upon to portray?

It is necessary to understand that his inner self, his imagination and emotion, generates an energy which is wholly desirable and from which all performance must spring. The difficulty arises when the body and voice do not respond to these inner impulses as immediately and flexibly as they should. A student will say: "That is how I wanted to play the character — I felt it but it wouldn't come out". So much gets in the way — the anxiety to do well, insufficient command of technical skills, which frustrate and inhibit. A body rigid with tension from fear, or a voice tight and restricted from the effort of pushing out towards the audience makes matters worse.

Although we are to examine in particular the effect of tension on the voice, it must be recognised that the voice cannot be considered in isolation. If the body is rigid the voice will reflect its rigidity. If the inner self is ill at ease because the part has been inadequately prepared, the essential emotional energy lacking, the voice has nothing to work on and it will sound empty and false, and the character seem superficial.

The student, therefore, must be encouraged from the beginning to see his body and his voice as an integral part of his inner self; that he must be free and responsive to all the demands, physical, mental and emotional, that this inner self, in its commitment to the character he is to play, makes upon him.

First let us consider a general daily preparation for the voice exercises to follow. This pattern of work must be practised from the start of training so that it becomes an essential part of the actor's and the operatic singer's background, much as barré exercises are to the ballet dancer.

Body limbering or warming-up

These exercises should encourage mobility of the spine and flexibility of the muscles and joints. They should not include exercises in strength for its own sake as this will create undesirable tension — Litz Pisk's recent book — *The Actor and his Body* — is a clear and excellent guide to the exercises most beneficial to the actor.

Limbering exercises completed, there follows a period on the floor when the actor may feel his body lengthening and widening, opening up, in fact, in preparation for the use of his voice.

a. Lie on the floor, on the back, the head supported by books; the span of the hand across the palm, fingers held together, will indicate the height, and number of books required.

b. Raise the knees, drawing the feet to a position a little forward of the knee and at a slight outward angle. The feet should be about eighteen inches apart.

c. Slip the hands, palms upwards, under the buttocks, and draw the back down towards the feet. The back should then be in contact with the floor.

d. In this position try to think of the body spreading out over the floor, like very soft dough or treacle. At the same time think of the back lengthening upwards, from the base of the spine right up through the neck and continuing into the head. The head should feel poised, a continuation of the neck and spine, rather like a ping-pong ball on top of the jet of water at the fair. Take time to feel the gradual freeing of the neck and the widening of the shoulders — the opening of the back and pelvis.

When the feeling of openness and freeing is established, proceed to the next exercise which is to free the back of the tongue and open the throat in preparation for use of the voice.

1. Keeping the mouth closed, allow a smile to grow inside the mouth at the back and feel the tongue free. Maintaining the feel of the smile, allow the jaw to open and sigh out on "AH". Be especially careful not to shorten the neck as the jaw is released.

2. Continue the smiling and release of jaw, and sigh out on the other vowels: "ER", "AY", "EE", "I" etc. Make sure they are all sighed out on a continuing outgoing breath, and check between each one that the feeling of the inside smile is maintained and that the neck is free and not shortening as the jaw opens.

3. Repeat the above exercise using words containing the vowel-sounds mentioned above, but unvoiced. Be aware of the constant flow of breath up through the body and out of the mouth as you sigh. Then repeat, but this time with voice. (It is not desirable at this stage to consider the intake of breath. It is the sensation of the outward flow of breath that frees; too much concern about the intake can cause tension through anxiety to have enough. It will be found, in any case, that after each sigh out the back will automatically spring open, thereby taking in another breath without any help from the student!)

4. The sighing exercise should now be repeated standing up.

From the recumbent position, roll over on to one side and curl up for a moment, knees drawn up to the chest. Then slowly sit up and finally stand. This precaution will prevent any feeling of faintness which a rapid move from lying down to standing may sometimes cause.

Before beginning the standing exercises, ensure that the back is open and free. This can be helped by allowing the knees to bend slightly and the pelvis to tilt forward (Dr. Barlow in his admirable book on the

Alexander Principle says "The genitals should always be worn to the front"). The body can then grow upwards from the hips as the knees are straightened (not braced) opening the back and giving a feeling of lightness.

Repeat the previous exercises first without voice, as before, then with voice, feeling the smile inside the mouth and checking to see that there is no shortening of the neck.

These are exercises which all student actors and opera singers should include in their daily programme and which will establish an awareness of the voice as part of the body. He will now feel the flow of the breath through the body, a body previously warmed up by the limbering exercises and he will have felt the vowels floated on the breath stream as he first sighs them and then speaks them out. He will have felt his body open and free and established a continued awareness of this as his voice floats on the breath. These exercises should be practised by singers, always aware of the breath stream which they use automatically in singing, but tend to cut off when confronted by the need for speech.

Keeping this awareness in his mind he may now proceed to using text. Nursery rhymes are an excellent introduction to more advanced text.

1. Whisper the words of any nursery rhyme on a continual flow of breath, feeling the rhythm and allowing the rhythm to dictate the need for further breath.

2. Now speak it aloud with confidence, feeling the flow of breath supporting the words and rhythm.

3. Now to strengthen the voice. Imagine the energy all around you and draw this energy into the lower part of the body. Then speak the lines again.

4. With the *intention* to speak the verse clearly in the

mind, and the feeling of energy flowing in and continuing to support the voice, speak it strongly and rhythmically right through, not allowing the energy to drop until *after* the last word is completed.

The knowledge that his voice can have strength and energy gives great confidence to an actor – he needs to feel what his voice is capable of, even though he may not always need that power, and confidence is a great antidote to tension. As the actor studies his part, the character begins to develop and come to life. He will have drawn on his imagination for an understanding of the character's emotions, of the intentions he has in anything he speaks, the reaction the character has to the situations he is placed in and the confrontations he experiences with other characters. As this confidence in the understanding and realisation of his character grows, so he needs to "feel" his character's voice. At this point, the inner energy and the outer energy must come together. His inner self has provided the fire to set the outer energy aflame. His inner self's conviction of, and the commitment to the character gives the right impetus to ignite the voice – tentatively at first perhaps, but with growing certainty, and if the body is free and the voice open and responsive, the voice will grow out of the character as the extension of the understanding within.

During the period of rehearsal, a disagreement or uncertainty may give a momentary check to this growth. Then the performer must in his mind recall the freeing exercises, remember and establish clearly in his mind again the intention his character has at that moment – and he will feel the return of confidence and a lessening of the tension the blockage has caused. If the preparatory exercises have been the basis of his work from the beginning, regularly performed and fully experienced, this recall of the feeling of openness will present no difficulty. The tension of the tongue which so often impedes the flow of breath, can be quickly released by the simple exercise of smiling inside the mouth and sighing out gently. A small, absolutely silent breath taken through the nose will help to free any tension in the back and shoulders, and allow the actor to compose himself before approaching his work again.

Away from rehearsal the actor should make use of his preparatory exercises to get the feel of his voice. Lying on his back in the recommended position he should bring to mind the character's intention in the speech he is about to speak, and, first whispering it, to feel the outward constant flow of breath, then speaking it with confidence, remembering as he does so the situation his character is in and what other characters are speaking, bringing to mind in fact, the whole scene he has been rehearsing.

A teacher can be of great help in assisting the student to use his energies in the right way — discussing with him his particular difficulties, pointing out where he may be obstructing the vital free flow of breath, either because physically he is not free or because he has not been clear in his evaluation of his character's intention.

But ultimately the artist is on his own and must create for himself the right climate for his work, adapting the exercises given here to his needs. Particular vocal exercises are not given here since they must be appropriate to the needs of the individual. No two voices are the same, so an exercise must be adapted to any special difficulty an actor may have. These can only be dealt with after a detailed diagnosis of the condition of the voice and the individual personality of the actor.

In preparing for performance the procedure is the same — first, a warm-up, then the freeing on the floor, establishing an awareness of the free flow of breath. The small silent breath as indicated before, taken through the nose, will help to establish this.

Most artists will like complete quiet before performance to go through their scenes silently as they make
up, finding in this process the confidence needed for
the performance. Others may find the tension of first-
night nerves too hard to bear and need to let off a
little steam, releasing some of the tension in this way
before they go on. A few find the excitement of meeting an audience for the first time so heady that they
only lose the tension as they walk on stage. How then
may one prescribe for such varying temperaments?
Only a solid basis of preparation, diligently performed
can give the necessary confidence. He will be accus-
tomed to the free sound of his voice.

A further note: In life we always want a response to
our actions or speech. Even our commands expect
obedience or reaction. We may not get the response
or reaction we expect. There ensues then a dialogue,
or possibly conflict, but all the time we make clear
and pursue our intentions. An actor has to divine by
analysis the intentions of the character he is to play
and he has to learn what reactions and responses that
character expects. He should ask then "What does
my character want and from whom?" If he places
himself at the centre and asks continually "What am
I feeling? What am I thinking?" he will find himself
pushing his character out towards the others (his voice
will become pushy as well) whereas if he considers
the other characters and their relationship to him,
and focuses attention on them, he will find his character
beginning to grow in depth and strength, his voice free
and his self-consciousness disappearing. "Awareness"
is surely the key to his problem of tension.

But first it is necessary to create a conscious awareness of self in order to counter the ill-effects which
self-consciousness brings:

a) Awareness of physical tension as a fact and a recognition of its presence and the form it takes with each individual,

b) the practise of appropriate exercises which will help to establish a 'norm' of freedom in body and voice,

c) the recognition of the free sound of the voice supported on the constant flow of the breath stream.

Above all, if an over-awareness of self is considered as a prime cause of tension, then the dispersal of interest from the self should result in greater freedom. It is towards this freedom, in preparation for the characters they will have to portray, that the actor and the operatic singer should strive.

The operatic singer's task is increased through his many responsibilities as a singer, an actor and an interpreter who must have command over the dialogue of that particular opera.

But if, with the breath as foundation, he can think of dialogue as an extension and continuation of the dramatic impulse which has been present in the music and will be present in the forthcoming music, his task will be made easier. It should be allowed the same energy that charged the sung line and should flow out of the music and into it again without any change of gear: singing voice and speaking voice should have the same quality and timbre. Naturally the content of the dialogue must be understood and related to the character and the dramatic situation, but once that is established , the singer's technique may be allowed to do the rest.

It is only through a profound study of these three facets of his role; voice, speech and interpretation that an opera singer's performance can become an organic whole.

NELLY BEN-OR

The Alexander Technique and Performance

Tension, according to the strict definition of the word, is a disruptive unwelcome element in performance. On the other hand no artistic performance should lack intensity. Unfortunately the two concepts — tension and intensity — only too often get confused and misunderstood. There is a tendency to believe that intensity cannot exist without tension but this is disputable.

Visible signs of 'strain and stress' in a performer may give a deceptive impression of intensity which may actually be lacking in the essence of the performance. Ferocious movements of the arms, 'impressive' shaking of the head, facial and bodily contortions in the performance of any artist — whether singer, instrumentalist or actor — do not mean that there is a real inner intensity in the artistic expression. Conversely some of the finest artists do not convey any impression of strain, even in performances of the highest intensity. This is a point I would like to take up in the light of practical experience as a concert pianist and as a teacher of both piano playing and the Alexander Technique. Although I am a musician it was from the work of a complete outsider to the world of music that I have learned much that has influenced my approach to the art of piano playing and performing.

After many years of formal training as a pianist and having gained experience of several different but well established methods of piano playing, I came across the work of Frederick Mathias Alexander — an educator in the widest sense of the word — who directs one's attention to the person as a psycho-physical whole. Alexander's work (known simply as the Alexander Technique) bears no specific relation to performance, whether of music or anything else. It has, however, a great deal to offer in the development of any individual's potential, often enabling him to increase his ability in various fields of activity and certainly has much to contribute to the art of piano playing.

I have always found it a challenging, yet somewhat frustrating task to speak or write about the Alexander Technique because the greater my experience of it the more I feel inclined to agree with the ancient saying: "the way that can be told is not the real way; the word that can be spoken is not the real word". Yet I have learnt the Technique and have been teaching it to others for many years now. Perhaps to say one "teaches" the Alexander Technique is not quite accurate. I would rather say that one guides a pupil towards a gradual but direct personal experience of the essence of it.

What I have learned from the Alexander Technique is not yet another specific instrumental method — one more to add to the many existing 'schools' of piano playing for instance — with their various approaches and exercises concerned with particular ways of using one's fingers, arms, wrists, weight, etc. All these direct the player's attention to one or more separate parts of the mechanism of piano playing without him considering these details in the context of himself as one indivisible whole. It is precisely this 'wholeness' of the player that should embrace and indirectly modify his approach, regardless of what the particular details of it are. If for example a piano method depends on curved fingers, another on them being kept flat, or on the hands being positioned in any particular way —

with the learning of the Alexander Technique each
of these details will acquire a new quality, another
dimension of freedom and unity of the whole person
playing. It is therefore possible for a pianist of any
technical schooling to gain much from the application
of the basic principle underlying Alexander's teaching.
May I add that this principle is equally valuable and
applicable to other forms of artistic performance,
whether in music, dance or drama, although as a pianist
I will understandably stress its relevance to piano
playing.

Before explaining what is Alexander's teaching it may
be of interest to learn who the man was and what led
to the evolution of his Technique.

Frederick Mathias Alexander was born in Tasmania
in 1869 and died in England at the age of 86. From
early childhood he was intensely interested in poetry
and by his late teens had established a considerable
reputation as a reader of poetry and professional status
as an actor. It was while engaged in this work in
Melbourne at the age of about 19 that he encountered
the problem which was to occupy him through the
next ten years or so and which would ultimately deter-
mine the direction of his life. The difficulty he developed
was a tendency for his voice to fail during recitals.
When the trouble began he went to doctors for help.
But the medical treatment afforded only temporary
relief. In time his condition became so aggravated
that Alexander often could not bring himself to accept
engagements as he felt uncertain of being able to get
through a full evening of reading. The climax was
finally reached when he lost his voice halfway through
an engagement which he regarded as particularly important to his career. Since his doctors found no medical
reason for his loss of voice, Alexander concluded that
it must be something he was doing which brought
about these disastrous results. It was that idea which

prompted him to embark upon a period of most careful and exacting observation of the way in which he used himself, particularly in the act of speaking. In the end he found this out and a great deal more besides.

Alexander discovered in the course of years of painstaking trial and error, through observation of himself and others, that there is a certain interaction between the head, neck and back, which determines the quality of our functioning as a whole. He termed it the Primary Control. He also observed that this Primary Control has a direct influence on the quality of any activity we engage in. Simple routine move- ments such as walking, sitting, or standing as well as more complex activities, as for example dancing or playing an instrument become infinitely more effort- less and light when one learns to do them without interfering with the subtle freedom in the head, neck and back interaction: the Primary Control. Alexander has pointed out, that after early childhood, there develops in almost each one of us an accumulative tendency to the wrong use of ourselves in the follow- ing way:

We generally tend to pull our head down and back into our neck (each individual in his own characteristic way) initiating a downward pressure, a collapsing influence on the rest of the spine and the whole body structure connected to it. For most of us this pulling down is so habitual that it does not feel wrong and usually becomes even stronger when we 'do' something — in other words we misuse ourselves most of the time, but particularly badly during any activity.

Alexander found that it was this habitual uncon- scious misuse of himself that caused him to lose his voice, and that a change and improvement in his use eradicated the problem completely. He also found that this downward pull and collapsing can be the cause of a variety of symptoms such as headaches, backaches, asthmatic conditions or a general lack of suppleness and lightness (which is so necessary for instance in playing an instrument). It is also a potent factor in states of depression and tension.

To eradicate these faults Alexander evolved a technique which initiates a process of freeing the neck and releasing the head away from the neck — slightly forward and up to encourage in turn a lengthening and widening effect on the torso. This results in a progressive releasing of accumulated, unnecessary tensions, and brings about an effortlessness and lightness in one's use, which one has hitherto not experienced.

Since this technique aims at changing fundamental habits of behaviour and reacting, one is taught first of all the ability to stop one's habitual reactions and gradually to replace them by new consciously directed ones. In a lesson of the Alexander Technique one does not learn how to do something (such as for example to get in and out of a chair, or to walk) but how to refrain from doing it and yet allow it to happen.

I know this sounds very mistifying to anyone who has never experienced it. But to those who work in the Technique (teachers and pupils alike) it is an everyday occurrence. This involves first of all learning how to leave oneself entirely in the hands of one's teacher. I mean it literally, because the teacher actually places his hands under the pupil's head and, gently releasing it from the neck, brings about a subtle freedom in the Primary Control, (i.e. in the head-neck-back relationship). One is then shown how this freedom is lost as soon as one attempts to do even the slightest thing. So, the next step is of course learning how to do something in a way that does not disturb the freedom of the Primary Control. It is possible to learn to do anything in this new way. Then throughout the activity the neck will remain free, the head will be released from the neck — so that there is no fixing or locking between them — and as a result of this the torso opens in length and width rather than collapses and contracts. Inevitably this has a positive influence on one's mental state too. An eminent doctor who became acquainted with the Alexander Technique once remarked to me that it made him acutely aware of the fact that no mentally disturbed or ill person shows any signs of good use or balanced bodily co-ordination.

The openness and freedom within the whole structure of the body is maintained by means of a conscious awareness, or 'thought directions' (to use Alexander's term), which brings one to realise the 'unity' of body and mind and so to experience a freedom of the whole self. The Alexander Technique points to a way of seeing oneself as a whole living being in whom details of use are inextricably bound up with a total pattern which functions best only when considered as a whole. The basic difference between Alexander's teaching and various other methods for improved co-ordination lies in the fact that through Alexander's approach one learns first of all how to eliminate habitual reactions and so discover within oneself new, quite different, ways of functioning. Lessons in the Alexander Technique are concerned with helping the pupil to learn how to stop 'doing' things and yet let them 'happen' through new unfamiliar means. The teacher is trained to communicate a change of alignment in the pupil's body through very gentle and skillfully guiding touch, but only when the pupil has understood the meaning of remaining quiet, or 'non-doing'. He may for example be asked to stand and only mentally project 'directions' to himself: "to let the neck be free, to allow the head to be released forward and up from the neck in order to let the back lengthen and widen."

While the pupil turns his attention to these 'directions' the teacher's hands bring about the corresponding effect in him. All this happens on a very precise but subtle level of sensory experience. When the meaning of mental 'directing' as opposed to physical 'doing' is understood and experienced, the pupil may be guided through a chosen activity while maintaining the same 'directions' so that the freedom which they produce is sustained throughout the activity. In other words the quality of openness and lightness does not give way to the strain habitually involved in 'doing' things. If for example one is sitting in a chair and mentally projecting the correct 'directions', the teacher will guide one from the sitting position into the movement of getting up in such a way that the effect of these 'directions', that is the freedom of the head-neck-back alignment, is not disturbed so long as the pupil's attention remains with the continuity of 'directing' not only before, but also during the act of getting up. Anyone who has experienced this will invariably react with amazement at the effortlessness of such a movement. I am of course trying to put into words a direct experience and this is attempting the impossible. No one can know the taste of wine without drinking it. A description can only tell us about the existence of something. What it really is can only be perceived by personal experience.

The practice of the Alexander Technique is based on three stages: inhibition, direction and activity (the terms used are Alexander's own).

i) *Inhibition of habitual reactions;* that is, stopping one's habitual responses and ways by not 'doing' the chosen activity. Instead:

ii) *giving mental directions;* that is, focussing one's awareness on "letting the neck be free, to let the head be released forward and up, to let the back lengthen and widen". These directions gradually replace the immediate habitual response towards doing things in the usual, often strenuous and mal-co-ordinated way. Then:

iii) *proceeding with the chosen activity while continuing the "directions" without interfering with them.* This is not easy at first because here one comes up against the most deeply ingrained habits of reactions. It may be relatively simple for anyone to let the Alexander 'directions' come into effect in himself, but the moment he is faced with having to do something his whole attitude changes. Just a mental readiness for an activity such as the thought "I am going to get out of the chair" results instantly in a locking of the head and neck, often also a tensing and hollowing of the back.

In some people these reactions may be only slight, but even the smallest degree of interference with the Primary Control alters the quality of one's functioning. That extra freedom in one's co-ordination disappears and varying degrees of strain and effort accompany whatever one does. I realise that much of what is taken for a normal level of tension and effort appears to be quite natural. However, when one experiences the possibilities of great freedom and ease inherent in ourselves, but dulled and distorted through wrong habits of use, one becomes aware of a new dimension of living and working without the commonly accepted level of strain.

In a lesson of the Alexander Technique the teacher may choose simple daily tasks (getting in and out of a chair, walking, etc.) as a background against which to illuminate the principle of Alexander's teaching. That principle relates however to the whole person and therefore to everything in his life. The physical and mental use of himself is affected and changed by it.

It takes a course of lessons to guide one towards a clearer awareness of the way in which one uses oneself as a whole in any situation of daily living and in relation to any activity. Walking, sitting down, getting up, moving an arm, speaking — in fact the whole range of automatic or semi-automatic activities — improve their quality when the Primary Control of the person is functioning well. Every aspect of the use of oneself gains mental and physical subtlety and is relieved from undue tension which is conventionally accepted as being unavoidable.

(Piano)

Turning to piano playing, it soon becomes apparent that much of the playing is bound up with strain, effort and undue waste of energy. This can bring about physical and mental fatigue and discomfort, which are obvious hindrances in performance. It is quite common to hear from even very accomplished performers, complaints of physical aches and discomfort as well as of mental strain in practising, and indeed performing.

By learning to incorporate into the mechanics of piano playing an improved use of the whole person, one gains freedom and ease in playing. In practical terms this means that everything in piano playing, from the movement of the hands towards the keyboard right through to the activity of the fingers in playing, can happen in such a way as not to interfere with the state of freedom between the head, neck and torso, so that a balanced co-ordination of the whole player is undisturbed. This can only be achieved through a thorough change in one's attitude towards ways of doing things generally. Such a change can take place gradually after one is shown to what extent we are governed by habits which influence all our psycho-physical functioning.

The Alexander Technique helps us to recognise our own fragmentation and dis-co-ordination in most things we do. This happens because we do not relate details of our activity to a total pattern of co-ordination. It comes as an amazing discovery to most people confronted in practice with Alexander's principle to realise that even simple activities such as for instance picking up a pen or walking a few steps invariably produce an instant stiffening and locking of the head, neck and back. An Alexander teacher can show a pianist for example that merely moving his hands towards the keyboard can cause this 'locking' which then increases when the playing begins. Part of the reason for this may often be that the player has insufficient knowledge of the text of the music he is playing. This, combined with so called technical difficulties which sections of the music may present, will become a real stumbling block in practising and build up totally avoidable tensions and problems.

In view of these facts, encountered by any practicing musician — student and professional alike — one can conclude that there could be two main starting points in the approach to practising which should lead to a clear and fluent performance: a) a thorough and clear learning of the text and b) bringing an awareness of the total use of oneself into practising. (I speak here as a pianist, but the same applies to any other player or performer).

a) The first point means getting to know the musical text preferably away from the instrument, learning it in the way a conductor studies his score or an actor his script. An inexperienced learner may begin by doing this in very short sections. The preliminary learning of a piece in this way without actually playing it may save time and prevent the player from getting into unnecessary difficulties, which often arise from attempting to practice a text with only a vague knowledge of it. It is surprising how much better one can understand and memorise a composition through such detailed quiet study. This kind of preparation is particularly useful if one wants to apply the Alexander principle to one's playing as a clear knowledge of the text which one wants to practise will automatically remove that part of disturbing tension which arises from the anxiety and uncertainty in practising a vaguely learnt piece.

b) The second point means incorporating in practising that extra awareness of the overall co-ordination in one's use. I must emphasise that this can only be learnt with the help of a skilled Alexander teacher who corrects and guides one into becoming aware of undue tension and distorting interferences in the head, neck and torso alignment; and so brings about an improvement in one's entire co-ordination. This is of vital importance in maintaining a freedom in the use of the player as a whole, adding a quite unusual degree of flexibility and ease in the use of his arms, hands and fingers. If one can experience in daily practising a greater simplicity and ease of playing one can complete the learning of a piece of music without any feeling of awkwardness or difficulty. I believe that one can only give a fluent performance of any piece of music when it does not 'feel' difficult; and this stage can, and should, be reached in any work one chooses to perform. Thus the destructive aspect of tension in performance can be eliminated to a very large extent and the Alexander principle, encompassing the whole person, will indirectly influence the details of his preparation for a performance.

A performer whose use of himself is well balanced, will not be disturbed by undue tension of the kind which is the result of effort and strain. He can, of course, choose to create tension deliberately, but that can be controlled and released at will. This kind of tension is not disruptive to performance because it does not just happen, but is used for a specific reason. I would prefer to call it intensity, or an increase in the flow of energy. However the term here is immaterial. What is important is the fact that within each one of us there exist sources of energy which can be used constructively and can be channelled so that a great deal of usual mental and physical stress and strain can be avoided, not only in artistic endeavours but also in all aspects of daily living.

This seems to be a daring claim, I know. But then so would be for instance the description of a radio, television or jet plane to a person living two centuries ago. Yet we take these 'miracles' for granted now. There are apparently miraculous possibilities within the depth of our own existence which Alexander's genius led him to discover. I say "apparently miraculous" because the changes in oneself which can be wrought through his Technique are of a very uncommon kind and may seem quite extraordinary. The Technique however is basically simple and points to a direct uncomplicated integration of a person. It is its very simplicity and directness which elude us at first because we are burdened by and dependent upon so many confused, disjointed and conflicting ideas and habits, without realising that it is possible at least to be shown a way of seeing them for what they are. The degree to which anyone will absorb Alexander's principle and function according to it will differ with each individual. It will depend on the extent to which he will be willing to give himself to a change of basic psycho-physical habits.

For any artist the self-knowledge which one can arrive at through the Alexander Technique would seem to be of inestimable value. And the freedom from disruptive tensions which the Technique affords can bring great relief and technical help.

CAROLA GRINDEA

Tension in Piano Playing
Its Importance and Dangers

It is perhaps significant for our society that so many people from all kinds of professions are continuously searching for some assistance in one particular direction: how to cope with the tension created by the strain of everyday existence, a strain which brings with it anxiety, insecurity and even distress.

Many people study Yoga disciplines, others join various meditation groups while quite a few are turning to 'Alexander Technique', the philosophy expounded by Matthias Alexander. All these disciplines and techniques demand regular study and exercises for a long period of time, involving continuous mental controls. The results are certainly worth while since so many people, from various walks of life, have been eager to testify.

For musicians, these are of real value. Though different in their approach, they have certain points in common, which are indispensable in performance: a balanced state of the body, a straight spine, freedom of breathing and a high degree of concentration – which at the same time allows the free flow of memory – again, qualities without which a performance cannot exist.

What about those – and they are a large majority – who do not believe it necessary to use their already limited time for studies other than music and how to become proficient at their instrument? After all, as so many musicians are arguing, the study of an instrument is in itself highly demanding, the player having to devote several hours every day on most exact and disciplined work to master that particular instrument and learn the repertoire. Similarly, other performers — actors, public speakers, dancers — are engaged in a programme of rigorous training, knowing that this is the only way to have control over their voice or body, the tools which would allow them to express their ideas and artistic ideals.

The strain imposed by this type of work, both physical and mental, is bound to generate a great deal of tension and, unless the player is able — consciously or unconsciously — to release it at certain moments, this can create serious problems.

A skilled performer instinctively maintains a perfect balance between generating and releasing tension, thus creating the illusion of continuous 'detente' in the same way as a film gives the illusion of continuous movement. What happens when an unaccomplished player uses antagonistic muscles or has not yet developed the ability to release between exertions? Well, there is anxiety and insecurity which cause nervous as well as muscular tension in many parts of the body, sometimes with very damaging effects.

What is tension? And why is it that so many evils of our society seem to be caused by it, from physical ailments to the inability of a performer to face an audience, to mention only these two extremes?

The Oxford Dictionary gives the following definition: ". . . effect produced by forces pulling against each other; highly strung state, maintenance of high degree of exertion; suppressed excitement", while the adjective 'tense' means: "stretched to tightness, strained or highly strung" — referring to "chord, muscle, nerves, eye". Well, this gives a clear picture of the havoc tension can cause if 'nerves, muscles, emotions are stretched beyond endurance'.

Tension, perhaps, may be compared to electricity. We cannot see it, we cannot touch it, yet it is there, it exists. If we can harness it the results are great, there is light, there is power. If not, it can become dangerously destructive. Like electricity, it has a positive and a negative side.

Let us look first at the positive aspect. *Tension is healthy.* It brings excitement and intensity to a performance without which no artist can communicate his ideas and his emotions to the listener. It is this communication which draws people to Concert Halls, in spite of occasional human imperfections which recordings succeed in eliminating through the repair work done in the studios. Which one of us has not known those moments of complete silence and intent expectation before a concert is about to begin, when the artist is alone with himself and his music? It is the tension created at such moments that heightens the qualities of a sensitive artist and makes each performance a unique experience.

In the same way, tension enhances creativity. A composer will be judged by the tension he brings in thematic development and interplay, or the intervallic tension of the melodic lines, while the harmonic and rhythmic structure come alive through that continuous urge towards climaxes.

What about the negative, destructive aspect? This presents a serious problem affecting the work of a musician both during his studies and in the performance.

Working with adult students and professional pianists I have become increasingly aware of the difficulties created by *too much tension* at *the wrong moment* and *in the wrong places.* Not only does this prevent the player to express himself with ease and use the keyboard with the necessary control but, what is more important, it affects the freedom of breathing, this essential biological function of the body.

There are students who take their work seriously, some with more natural ability than others, devoting several hours every day to the study of their instrument. Quite a few are fine musicians, with real grasp of the intellectual content of the work and showing great respect and understanding for the composer's style, and trying to read beyond his markings of phrasing, dynamics or tempi. They know what they wish to convey to the listener, yet there is this barrier between their body and the instrument which prevents them from expressing their ideas or their intentions.

There are also those who believe that they understand the meaning of relaxation at the piano, sometimes getting over-relaxed, or at other times unable to maintain that state for longer periods, particularly when the music demands great agility, ample sonorities and stamina.

On the other hand there are some — very few indeed — who seem to possess a superb inner rhythm and an intense inner hearing which almost always prompts the right movements, producing the desired response from the instrument. They also have an uncanny ability to combine the moments of great tension with those of repose, making everything look as if piano playing is a natural function. From these few I have learnt a great deal.

I started to take notes observing the different stages of their performances hoping to discover something about the various reactions of each player, particularly to find out how and why tension affects some players more than others. This was no easy task.

I turned to the Libraries. There I found a spate of books on Piano Technique, which were of two kinds. *Technique A - B* On the one hand, those with endless exercises on how to practise the different 'technical aspects' of piano playing (which Heinrich Neuhaus so aptly dubbed the 'prefabricated material' for pianists) and on the other, those which examine and theorise about the various *'aspects of piano technique'*.

It appears that, for centuries, pedagogues and keyboard players have been obsessed with the best way to obtain finger agility as the means to all ends. From the first treatises, the Fundamenta for organ and early keyboard instruments — printed at the end of the 15th century — up to the beginning of the 20th century when certain schools advocated that pianists should dispense with this type of training, the accent has been on exercising the five fingers of each hand for hours, every day, for many years, as the only road to proficiency.

One only has to study *Methode des Methodes* which Francois Fétis, the Belgian pedagogue and musicologist of the last century — published in Paris in 1837 — to realize that every pianist of repute has written his 'own method'. Fétis gives detailed descriptions comparing the most important methods hitherto published, with their specific fingerings and dogmatic sets of technical exercises. With his generous humour, Fétis sums up the different methods, concluding that although some of the approaches to similar technical problems are almost poles apart, there must be some truth in each one and the unequivocal statements that 'this is the only way to play the piano' have undoubtedly been proved by the masterly performances of everyone of these pianists *and* of their pupils!

No one denies the value of regular study of technical exercises — as a means to an end, that is the expression of artistic ideals — as long as these exercises *are not conflicting with natural movements and do not create unnecessary muscular tension.*

The other type of books, by eminent pedagogues and authors, examine the vast subject of Piano Technique from every possible angle. Is Piano Technique an art? Is it a science? I give here a few titles for the sake of argument.

Book

The Natural Piano Technique by Rudolf M. Breithaupt (C.F. Kant Nachfolger, Leipzig 1905)

The Science of Piano Technique by Thomas Fielden (MacMillan, London 1927)

The Art of Piano Playing — A Scientific Approach by George A. Kotchevitsky (Sammy Birchard, Co. New York 1967)

The Art of Piano Playing by Heinrich Neuhaus (Barry Rockliffe 1975)

Zur Psychologie der Klaviertechnik by Willy Bardas (Werk Verlag, Berlin 1927)

The Physical Basis of Piano Touch and Tone by Otto Ortmann (Kegan Paul, N.Y. Dutton 1925)

The Physiological Mechanics of Piano Technique by Otto Ortmann (Kegan Paul, N.Y. Dutton 1925)

The Indispensables of Piano Playing by Abby Whiteside (New York Coleman-Ross 1955)

There are many more, which indeed are quite enough to confuse any young student in search of some truths. And recently, the latest addition, *Famous Pianists and their Techniques,* a monumental book by Reginald R. Gerig (David & Charles, 1976) examining *all* the methods and schools of piano technique up to the present time.

Some of the theories and discoveries put forward in these books have certainly opened new vistas and shed new light regarding the understanding of the complex physical and physiological processes involved in piano playing. It is only due to these pioneers that we understand how our musical computer works inside the brain, receiving well programmed information, and sending, through very slight impulses from the central nervous system, directives to our peripheric apparatuses for the correct (or more or less correct) movements. We even believe that we understand how our kinesthetic sense works, or, in plain language, how the so-called muscular memory manages to take our different parts of the playing apparatus in the right directions at the right moment, through 'conditioned reflexes'.

We, pianists, owe a great debt to pedagogues like Tobias Matthay, who, in his magnum opus *The Act of Touch* (published as early as 1903, in London) not only presented an analytical and systematic study of the physical and physiological aspects of piano technique, but was the first theoretician to give a scientific explanation of the mechanical laws of the instrument, thus making it clear how to 'connect' the two sides, the player and the instrument. He has also established the meaning of 'relaxation' at the piano, that state of balance when the elastic and harmonious muscular condition of the playing apparatus prevails, and every single joint is free. Like the other 'relaxationists' — Ludwig Deppe, around 1870, in Germany, had already expounded his theories on the relationship between controlled arm weight and beauty of tone — Matthay in England, Breithaupt in Germany and Marie Jaëll, in France, advocated the use of controlled arm weight in piano playing. This has made *one of the greatest contributions as regards the release of muscular tension in performance*.

It was to be expected that other pedagogues, in search of new truths, would present various new discoveries, attacking the previous ones. Thus Otto Ortmann, through extensive laboratory tests and measurements, at Peabody Conservatory, in Baltimore, has been able to prove that arm weight is never used at the moment of tone production, even though the pianist is convinced that he is experiencing it. (*The Physiological Mechanics of Piano Technique*).

What matters — and particularly for our study — is the fact that the player *experiences* release of muscular tension through conscious use of arm weight, in spite of the scientific evidence that this is actually happening only *before* and *after* tone production! After all, not only the body but also the mind should be free of tension and surely the imagination plays a vital role in creating in the player's mind the illusion that he is experiencing the continuous use of the arm-weight — which can only be achieved if the body is in a state of so-called 'relaxation' at the piano. In the same mysterious way *Legato!* that same illusion is also transmitted to the listener. After all, pianists *can* play legato and the listeners hear legato sounds, even though scientific experiments deny the possibility of obtaining legato tones from the instrument.

Far from attempting to expound here the qualities or faults of the many and sometimes opposed theories and discoveries, I am concerned here only with certain aspects of piano playing which present some answers as regards the release of tension in performance.

After studying a great number of books, one big question remains unanswered.

How is it that with all the knowledge and the comprehension of the very complex actions and reactions in piano playing, there are still so many pianists suffering from the effect of tension, and this vital problem regarding the player and the performance of music remains unsolved?

It is true that a great deal of research has been and is still being done in many Psychiatric Units and Departments of Psychology at various universities to study the ways in which tension can attack our mind, our body, in fact our whole being. Do these experiments and analyses cast more light on our search? Only in so far as we are told that tension exists, that through highly sensitive instruments it can be measured and the slightest changes in brain impulses can be registered.

What concerns us, musicians and performers in general, is to learn something about the causes of tension and its effects, and particularly how these affect

? Take a different tack ??

other forms of relaxation learning (M Brusar)
which then impact on piano playing etc

the player during the performance. Paradoxically
enough it is only by observing the effects that we can
arrive at an understanding of the causes. Also, the
greatest obstacle in our study is the fact that no one
is quite certain at which particular point *the tension-
effect becomes itself a cause.* The chemistry of the
human body remains one of the great mysteries of
nature and, although we do know that much of the
work is done by the unconscious mind, through involuntary actions, we are very far from knowing how to
control them. Since tension is the result of involuntary
actions which are beyond our control, we can only
become aware of its power and existence within ourselves.

A. INNER NERVOUS TENSION

In studying the causes and effects of tension we must
differentiate between the INNER NERVOUS TENSION
— which may be the result of *mental* and/or *emotional*
stress — and MUSCULAR TENSION of the playing
apparatus, which may have *physical* or *physiological*
causes due to the pianist's lack of skill. The two types
of tension *cannot be isolated; they react upon each
and there is a continuous and almost simultaneous
interplay.* The slightest hesitation or emotional anxiety
during the performance creates inner nervous tension
(the player becomes aware of this mainly in the solar
plexus area — a centre of nervous tension), which is
almost simultaneously transmitted to various parts of
the body — usually to the weaker parts of the playing
apparatus — causing muscular tension. And vice-versa,
when the player experiences some difficulties, whether
maintaining an exertion for too long or using antagonistic muscles, not only muscular tension will be generated but also extra nervous tension will be there, affecting the quality of the performance.

On the positive side, nervous tension finds expression

in the intensity of the performance and the deeper the emotional involvement of the artist, the greater the intensity of the performance.

On the negative side, mental and emotional stress will create a state of anxiety which in turn will build up a high proportion of nervous tension, very often with serious implications. We cannot approach the sensitive area of mental and emotional tension without trespassing on the field of psychological research. Yet, music teachers are expected to be not only good pedagogues but also to have an understanding of the psychological problems of their students, to be capable of steering them through any crisis that might arise.

Mental anxiety must bring with it mental tension — which is both *cause* and *effect*. Perhaps the student is suffering from lack of confidence and he is unduly worried while the fear of an unsuccessful performance weighs heavily on his mind. If the pieces studied are beyond his intellectual grasp or his technical ability, his anxiety will not allow him to concentrate on anything else and naturally his work will suffer and sometimes his health may be affected. The decision rests with him, either to leave the pieces for a later date and choose others which will not tax his abilities, or accept the challenge, and carry on. It is interesting to witness the changes which such a renewed determination can bring in a musician's attitude towards conquering his problems. Here again is one of the positive aspects of tension.

Mental exhaustion goes hand in hand with *emotional stress*, though the causes might be brought about by experiences outside the musical sphere. Basically, it is fear at the root of this state, fear of failure or of being hurt. Perhaps the player is under excessive pressure from his family or he is unable to establish relationships with friends and colleagues or just with one person. At other times, he might find himself worn out by the competition in the musicians' world — to mention a few situations with which most of us are familiar. Unfortunately, the highly sensitive students are the most vulnerable. Here again, it is up to the student to learn to face his problems. However, continuous encouragement and constructive criticism from an understanding teacher, or some friendly help and advice from colleagues, can do wonders in many cases and the pianist might come to see the reality in a different perspective and even come to terms with it.

We cannot stop at these considerations of a psychological nature, no matter how relevant they are to our study. We must pursue the matter further and examine how a pianist suffering from mental or emotional stress can learn to release some of the nervous tension, which otherwise might affect, or even ruin, his performances.

If one observes pianists who perform with more ease than others one can notice that there is an amazing *coordination* between the movements of their body and the music, and there is a superb timing as regards tone production. The freedom of breathing is there, unhindered, giving the necessary expanse to the performance.

1. Coordination Between the Inner Rhythm and the Musical Rhythm

This coordination is a paramount condition if a musician is to attain *an equilibrium between generating and releasing tension* during the performance. A musical student instinctively sways his body with the musical rhythm (not the metric one!) and breathes at the right moment. These movements are hardly visible, not like exaggerated ones which may have no relation whatsoever with the music played and which are the expression of conflicting tendencies or the player's lack of skill. The swaying of the body, when the performer is identifying himself with the work, appears as if it takes place right inside the pianist, who, by intensely living the inner sound and the rhythm, gives expression to his emotions through movements *which seem organically grown,* obtaining from the instrument every possible kind of tone, shade or colour. These movements are healthy and conducive towards that much sought after equilibrium. They are also *energy generating,* and help to build up the player's stamina, that power to sustain a performance, and though he is emotionally exhausted he does not experience physical fatigue. It is a known fact that standing completely still for a long time can be extremely tiring, while even very slight oscillations of the body have the effect of increasing its resistance. A conductor — or, for that matter, any performer facing an audience — can stand for hours on the podium, just because his body is moving in complete accord with the musical rhythm of the works, *creating tension* and *releasing it* at the right moment.

The best illustration is Arthur Rubinstein's great discovery when crossing the Atlantic for the first time and the ship 'began to dance in the most alarming way'. After two long nights of being continuously seasick, he dragged himself upstairs and started to play the piano. He found that he was feeling better and the playing went quite well. "I made a brilliant discovery: when playing a piece which had a strong rhythm *I would breathe with that very rhythm* and not with the heavy, irregular up and down movements of the ship, which make one so promptly seasick." (*My Young Years,* page 171.)

Can one learn or acquire this coordination?
The answer is that it *is* possible to learn it and, if a student does not achieve it instinctively, he must strive towards its realization.

Nervous inner tension seems to invade the body and the mind of the player from and in so many directions, like an octopus with an endless number of tentacles, that we must confront it from as many directions as possible. As it acts primarily on the player's breathing, we have to study ways and means to maintain the free flow of breath.

Freedom of Breathing

The pianist should sit as comfortably as possible, studying his posture, and do the following simple exercise, which aims at releasing inner tension in the solar plexus area, one of the centres of nervous tension.

   a) breathe in − slowly, counting 1, 2.
   b) hold breath − without tensing the body, counting 1, 2, 3, 4.
   c) breathe out − slowly counting 1, 2.

(This should be taught from the very first piano lesson − or any music lesson − so that a young pupil experiences the sensation of 'let-go', not just being told to relax!)

This breathing exercise should be practised regularly, before starting the daily studies, and without fail, before a performance. The player will become aware of a sensation of freedom and should be able to recall that sensation as often as possible during the performance. There is no need, and certainly, no time, to do the whole exercise during playing, but he must *exhale*, slowly, from time to time. Through one simple exhalation, a performer gets all that is needed to counteract the effects of tension: the upper part of the torso becomes free, the back and neck are loose, the shoulders have dropped miraculously, the arms are hanging on each side of the body, yet they feel light and poised, the arm weight is transmitted to the hand and knuckles, while the fingers also receive a measure of the arm weight, supporting it, ready to pass it on to the keys.

All that remains is to add the required energy to produce the tone he wishes to hear from the instrument. At the same time, both inner and muscular tension have been released. *One slight exhalation, acting on the diaphragm,* is quite sufficient to unleash such complex reactions, so vitally linked with the quality of the performance and with the well-being of the pianist. *If only more importance were given to freedom of breathing in piano playing (and in teaching) many of the problems created by tension would solve themselves.*

Educating the Inner Hearing

a) Singing or humming the melodic lines and phrases — is essential. C.P.E. Bach wrote: 'The best way to feel the natural flow of a phrase is to sing it.' (in *Essays on the True Art of Playing Keyboard Instruments*) Not enough emphasis is placed on the value of learning to hear the score inwardly, studying it away from the instrument, observing the structure of the work, the phrases as they succeed each other leading to climaxes and noticing where the cadences occur. What is important though, is *to sing or hum melodic lines* to realize where each phrase ends, and *where one should breathe* and particularly where the player was — so to speak — going against the music, by inhibiting his breathing.

Singing should be part of the training of pianists, or for that matter of any instrumentalist, in order to develop the ability to hear the music inwardly.

b) Listening to the tone mentally — is closely connected with the player's faculty of hearing the music inwardly. First, he must study the work and then, in order to give a fine rendering, he must learn to hear each tone in his imagination. 'By developing the inner hearing we act directly on the tone production, and vice versa, by striving to produce better and better quality of tone has a direct influence on perfecting the inner hearing.' (Heinrich Neuhaus in *The Art of Piano Playing*.)

The link between the inner hearing and the movements prompted in piano playing has been the subject of several important studies, from Marie Jaëll's — a pupil of Liszt — *L'Intelligence et le Rhythme dans les Mouvements Artistiques* (Paris 1904) and Beatte Ziegler's *Das Innere Hören als Grundlage einer Natürlichen Klavier Technik* (Berlin 1925) to more recent times, Abby Whiteside's *Indispensables in Piano Playing* (New York 1955) or Heinrich Neuhaus' *The Art of Piano Playing* (London, 1975) while the violinist Kato Havas in *Stage Fright* (London 1975) expresses similar ideas. In fact, all these great pedagogues have worked towards finding some answers to the complex problems of coordinating the movements of the player with the musical rhythm of the works.

Study where Rhythmical and Musical Accents are in the score and play these with a *downward* exertion of the wrist (this will be discussed in detail in the section on *Muscular Tension*) — and *breathe out* at the same time. It is through these downward attacks of the wrist, in response to the music, that the pianist achieves the coordination which he is trying to acquire.

This conscious attention to breathing is necessary *only* when practising. In performance there is no need as *all downward exertions of the wrist are accompanied by a downward movement of the diaphragm,* through an exhalation which is hardly perceptible even to the player himself — (one of those invisible actions inherent in piano playing!)

Observing the Breathing while Playing *in Learning/Practice*
The pianist should play slowly, part of his programme at a time, consciously observing his breathing, and particularly taking notice at what point he is taking a

deep breath or he stops breathing. As tension affects the freedom of breathing, he must learn to breathe naturally and freely in preparation for and during the performance. We all know that moment of anxiety when playing a so-called difficult passage, when one stops breathing and once the danger point is over the player sighs heavily.

The best way to overcome this is by slowly *exhaling* before starting that tricky passage, and play it, being aware of the lungs getting gradually filled with air. There will be no more inner tightenings and the pianist will be surprised to find that he can play with ease and the figuration was not that difficult after all! He should play it several times, with the same attention to breathing, and thus he will gradually gain the confidence that he has conquered one of the difficulties encountered.

What happens, in fact, is quite simple. The knowledge that there are certain points in the score which he approaches with hesitation, or even anxiety, is bound to create nervous tension, which, in turn acts on the breathing, and the player stops breathing altogether. But by breathing out just before these awkward bars nervous and muscular tension is eliminated and the pianist feels quite free, while his fingers and arms move with unexpected ease.

There is no need to discuss or think about breathing in. Naturally, after exhaling, one has to breathe in. But, after inhaling, one can hold the breath for a very long time, and this is just what a player should *not* do, during the performance.

This conscious study of breathing when playing should be done *only when practising*. During the performance, the player should just *breathe out from time to time,* experiencing a sensation of well-being, free of mental and muscular tension. The breathing in will look after itself, and while he is slowly inhaling, his mind and body are somehow getting recharged with the necessary energy to cope with the work in hand.

Playing the Pieces Mentally while in a State of Physical Relaxation
Various methods of achieving physical relaxation are now common knowledge and these are practised in many fields of activities. For the musician, the real work begins at this stage. While lying on his back, completely relaxed, the pianist should go through the pieces, imagining that he is giving a performance. He will observe that every moment of intensity is accompanied by just as powerful inner tightenings, mostly in the diaphragm area. He should go again through the same passages, watching that the body is not actively involved, otherwise too much tension is created without any outlet.

This intellectual exercise demands acute and continuous concentration, but the results are certainly very important, as the power of concentration and the ability to memorize the works are greatly developed. One must add that inner tension is released through correct and free breathing while the body is in this state of relaxation.

B. MUSCULAR TENSION OF THE PLAYING APPARATUS
For a better understanding, we are studying the two types of tension separately, though we are, in fact, concerned with their interplay and how this affects the performers. So far, the accent has been on inner tension and how to release it at certain moments. *Since inner tension is not an isolated phenomenon and is always accompanied by muscular tension* in many parts of the body, it is obvious that the *reverse will also happen and when muscular tension is created, inner tension will inevitably result.* Therefore, if we *learn to release muscular tension this will also have the right effect on nervous tension.*

Muscular tension in the playing apparatus, when not caused by nervous tension, is created by physical and physiological causes, usually as a result of the player's lack of skill. In fact, it is easier to cope with muscular tension if the pianist or the teacher makes a study of the physical and physiological processes inherent in piano playing and works towards mastering a piano technique based on natural, well-coordinated movements.

As far as our study is concerned, I will only discuss here the movements needed in piano playing *which bring release of tension,* and which can be executed with the minimum amount of tension.

We must study this type of tension in two stages: 1) **Static Stage** and 2) **When setting in motion the playing apparatus.**

NB

1. The *Static stage* includes: a) breathing exercises, and b) posture.

By *Static* we understand the stage preliminary to the performance, when the pianist sits in front of the instrument and prepares himself for that extraordinary moment when he has to begin. What does he do? He makes himself as comfortable as possible, takes a few deep breaths, and concentrates on the music he is going to perform. It is irrelevant whether he belongs to a school which believes in a high seat or to one which is convinced that only a low seat can provide the player with the requisites to become an outstanding performer. All that matters is that he should feel at ease and enjoy the height of the stool which gives him the assurance that he can control the keys.

a) The *Breathing Exercise* which is discussed in the chapter INNER TENSION should be done before the performance. These long exhalations, followed by slow intakes of air have a quietening effect and the player must be aware of this happening. No pianist should start to play until his body is in a state of poise without any strain or tension, and this certainly can be achieved mentally and physically and also through the breathing exercise.

b) (*Posture*) is of paramount importance in performance. Bad posture can be one of the causes of accumulated tension in many parts of the body and it is worth mentioning that all the great pedagogues along the centuries have insisted on a 'good posture' as a foundation for a well-coordinated piano technique.

What is 'good posture'? The pianist can discover for himself what a good, natural posture is. When breathing out, the body is in a *state of balance,* the tensions are evenly distributed, with only muscle tone present; the neck and the back are not tight, the shoulders have dropped, the arms are hanging loosely, as if floating from a light anchorage at the shoulders, while the hands and fingers − in playing position over the keyboard − are receiving some of the arm weight. (See *Inner Tension*)

> "The organist or harpsichordist should sit in such a manner that his body is in the middle of the keyboard. He must sit still, holding his head erect, in a graceful posture. He must pay attention that the arm leads the hand which must be at a right angle to the arm, neither lower, nor higher . . . . The fingers, slightly curved, over the keyboard, must be prepared ready to play . . . The hand must be held *without tension* over the keyboard, lightly, as if stroking a child's head, otherwise the fingers cannot move with precision and agility."

Thus wrote Girolamo Diruta, in *Il Transilvano or Dialogo sopra il vero modo di sonar organi e instrumenti da penna* (Dialogue on the right manner of playing the organ and plucking instruments) in one of the earliest texts, published in 1593 or 1597. (Weitzmann-Seifert: *Geschichte der Klaviermusik,* p. 41, Breitkopf & Härtel, Leipzig, 1899)

No change as regards posture since the 16th century, or hardly any. Since the grand piano and the music make greater demands on the player, it is imperative that he should become more aware of the muscular condition of his whole body and of the sensation of the arm-weight, learning to make use of it, to produce fuller sonorities from the instrument.

Legs and feet must not be neglected. The right foot should be brought forward by the damper pedal, the player occupying only two thirds of the seat so that his *centre of gravity* falls in front, between his legs, not at the back. The abdomen and the lower dorsal muscles must be firm, as these have to support the upper part of the body, which must be free to move from one end to the other of the keyboard.

If the posture is correct, the pianist should become aware of the weight of his arms in the elbows. He must then *imagine* the arms becoming light without changing their position. This mental exercise is possible due to the fact that, when bent, the arms *feel* lighter than when they are stretched or hanging down, as the same weight is evenly distributed.

What about hand position? All schools of piano technique agree that hand position is important as a basis for good piano playing. Some schools demand prominent finger-knuckles, while others insist on a loose, flat hand.

Let the pianist study the shape of his hand when completely free of tension, away from the instrument. He will notice that the fingers hang loosely from the knuckles, which are quite prominent. Why not accept this natural hand position as a basis for piano playing? Such a position allows free movement of fingers, the thumb has ample room to pass under the hand, and, the hand can easily pass over the thumb.

The pianist is now ready to go to the next stage: 2. *Setting in motion the playing apparatus.* This is conditioned by very complex physical and physiological processes which have been analysed and dissected in great detail by a number of pedagogues (Matthay, Ortmann, Schultz, and others).

Playing the piano does not mean using only fingers, hands and arms. The whole body is involved and that is why the state of balance should be continuously maintained, otherwise a great deal of tension will be created in many parts. The muscular coordination of the human body is such that the slightest movement involves a whole chain of muscles, which have to contract, relax and balance at the precise moment, or reverse their action with the same lightning speed. Therefore, every pianist must practise *economy of movement*, avoiding unnecessary exertions and concentrate only on those essential to the performance. Moreover, these motions should be executed 'correctly' — that is *based on natural position permitted by the ossature and musculature of the playing apparatus*, maintaining the elasticity of the joints.

Correct Mental Process and Release of Muscular Tension

Before examining the movements of the various units of the playing apparatus which are conducive to piano playing with minimum of effort and maximum of efficiency, I should like to point out how a pianist can acquire this through a very simple *mental process*.

Whether the pianist uses the high articulation technique, with bent fingers, in the true 19th century 'Stuttgard tradition' or the straight and flat fingers of the so-called Russian school, or the thrusting, bent fingers for brilliant touch according to Matthay's teaching, or indeed, perfecting the use of the first phalange of the finger, in a 'scraping' movement, all these — prepared or unprepared touches — *can* and *should* be executed with a minimum amount of tension. More than that. All volumes and shades of tone, and all different touches: pressing the keys fast or gradually, maintaining the pressure or just holding the keys down lightly, using energy or weight — can be realized with ease, only if the player understands and masters the mental process which helps to release the tension created in preparation and at the moment of tone production.

Most pianists find it quite strenuous to think: *release after contractions,* particularly in passages requiring speed and tonal intensity. But, by reversing the mental process, the pianist is able to cope with all the problems which previously have caused him difficulty and anxiety. This is how it works:

If a pianist realizes that only a minute fraction of a second is needed to produce any kind of tone, he will also realize that all he has to do is to concentrate on maintaining the balance of the arms and body, which he then *interrupts* just for *that split second.* This is so infinitesimal that the arms and the body have no time to change, so to speak, their configuration, and the state of balance appears to be continuing or even seems *to gain in continuity.* This process is analogous to that of Morse Code signalling apparatuses — with the only difference that the machine does not have to think while the pianist must be all the time on the alert, aware of his muscular condition. Here is another situation when the player experiences a continuous state of freedom of his body which scientifically cannot be accepted. Does this matter? Certainly not. It is more important that he should feel at ease and be able to control his movements.

This mental process is of immeasureable value to the performer. At the same time, though, the pianist should study certain movements needed in piano playing which are conducive to release of muscular tension, or, at any rate, can be executed with the minimum of tension.

a) *Finger movements* should be initiated at the knuckles

knuckles, in a gripping action — the first movement of a baby's hand — when only the 'small muscles' situated inside the palm are involved. These act on the first joint (the nearest to the knuckles) which in turn pulls the other two. Since all schools of piano technique admit that there must be finger action, why not concentrate on this type of action? The player should study these movements of fingers to verify for himself which are the ones which cause less tension. He will find that if the fingers are exaggeratedly curved, the forearm muscles enter in action, but, almost straight fingers can be raised with hardly any tension.

In passages of agility, the action becomes almost invisible, the fingers are pulled very fast in the direction of the palm, and if the wrists and arms are free of tension, their movements will become complimentary, and the wrists will be free to vibrate.

All the great players and pedagogues who have written their 'Methods', from the 16th century up to the beginning of our century have insisted on finger articulation, from the knuckles, yet they have all stressed the importance of using *finger movements without tension in the wrist or arms*. Kalkbrenner, the great virtuoso of the first part of the 19th century, even perfected a *'Guide-Mains'*, which supported the wrists and forearms while the player was doing his exercises, developing the independence of fingers, which enables him to draw great volume of tone from the piano *without effort or tension*. (Kalkbrenner's *Method for Teaching Piano, with the help of the Hand-Guide*, Paris 1830). Who knows? Perhaps the 'relaxationists' might never have had reasons to expound their theories, had the second and third-rate pedagogues read more carefully the clear and precise observations on this point, and would not have caused so much damange to generations of pupils forced to practise for hours those exercises with stiff wrists and forearms!

b) The wrists play a most important role in the work of counteracting unnecessary muscular tension, and pianists should give great consideration to their complex roles and diversity of movements.

1. The wrist acts as point of fixation in preparation and at the moment of tone production, but it must revert constantly to its state of balance, regaining suppleness, to be able to execute the necessary movements, in so many directions. (See *Correct Mental Process*)

2. It acts as a bridge, allowing the arm weight to be transmitted to the hand and fingers.

3. It executes a diversity of motions in many directions; vertical — downward and upward; horizontal, in two directions; rotating — supination and pronation; circular movements — first described by Liszt, who coined the term 'cycloidal' — a downward curve or an upward one, sometimes a complete circle. These *eight directions of* wrist motions should be thoroughly studied and understood so that the pianist should have a clear mental picture of their execution.

4. The wrist is also acting in a *vibrato motion*, in passages of great velocity or very fast octaves — only when the player is applying the 'mental process' analysed in the previous paragraph.

Vertical Wrist Motions

Through vertical wrist motions, the pianist is able to bring about that vital coordination between the body, music and instrument.

The *Downward Exertion* (should be marked in the score, like a downbow for string players) — for masculine endings, rhythmical accents, chords demanding tonal intensity, etc.

The *Upward Motion* — a 'thrust' of the wrist, bringing the whole arm with it, for powerful chords of short duration, staccato octaves, etc.

There is another *Upward Motion* — a light upward movement of the wrist, catching the key on the way; for feminine endings, light staccato passages, short chords followed by a long, powerful one, also for the short moments of rest in the phrase.

In preparation for a powerful downward exertion, the pianist should bring the upper arm and the wrist into the position allowing the greatest amount of weight.

According to Ortmann's experiments, it is the one with 'high wrist and upper arm extending forward at a slight descending angle'. The wrist is then brought down with the needed energy, concomitantly with the whole arm and shoulders.

During practice, it is advisable that the player should *consciously exhale* at this moment. There is no need to do this during the performance as the diaphragm is pushed upwards, without the player being aware.

NB

One word of warning is necessary: these downward movements must not be exaggerated, the wrist must not descend more than half to one centimetre and the hand must not collapse. Knuckles and fingers remain *firm, forming a bridge* to receive the impact of the energy and weight, as well as acting as the point of contact between this impact and the key resistance.

Cycloidal Wrist Motions

If the player's arms are free of tension, the wrists are continually doing some 'undulatory' movements — which are hardly noticeable. In response to the music, the wrist will draw either a downward curve or an upward one. Liszt was the first pianist to become aware of these curvilinear movements of the wrists. He observed Chopin's playing during a recital and he was quite surprised to notice that the wrists were also doing almost imperceptible motions, 'in waves' — as he described them. He realized that there must be a connection between Chopin's exquisite quality of tone and these motions. Yet, it is hardly understandable how this was possible when the training at that time was fanatically rigid, demanding complete immobility of hands and arms. Liszt himself, in his young days as a teacher, occasionally placed two large books under the pupil's arms to stop them from moving. But later on, his teaching took completely new directions, his circle of disciples at Weimar having to study the 'cycloidal' wrist motions. These laid the foundation of the modern piano technique, demanding complete freedom of arms and wrists, allowing the arm weight to be transmitted or withdrawn when necessary.   *In Practice*

Since these motions are 'natural' and an integral part of piano playing, no pianist can afford to ignore them. He should study them until they have been mastered and have become an inherent part of his playing and then he should look at the score to realize where these should be applied.

In performance, however, he must allow the wrist motions to 'happen' and they certainly will, if the arms and the body balances are not interferred with.

Wrists in Repose

How right Leschetitzky was when he compared a 'singer's deep breathing with the pianist's muscular relaxation'! I take this statement further. *The wrist is the pianist's second breathing organ.* The playing apparatus can 'breathe', during those infinitesimal moments between exertions, when *the wrist is in repose, raised high, with the hands hanging loosely.*

This is the position of the wrist for just a fraction of time when a skilled pianist 'breathes' between phrases.

This is the position of the wrist when he shifts his arms and hands from one chord to another, along the keyboard, creating curvilinear movements, not jerky ones.

This is the position of the wrist, acting as a pivot, when the player has to perform big skips with one hand. Paradoxically, if the wrist is high, the distance between the two extremities appears shorter.

And finally — with very few exceptions, in very staccato passages — the pianist takes his hands off the keys, *slowly raising his wrists first*, bringing the hand and fingers after.

Needless to add that these movements or moments of stillness have been studied in 'slow motion'. A skilled pianist has arrived at them, instinctively, through his need to maintain the continuous balance between creating and eliminating tension. But, every player can and should acquire them, by studying them consciously for a while, until they have become conditioned reflexes.

c) Arms and Shoulders

The arms and the shoulders have been discussed all through this essay. As to the arms, it is essential that the student should learn to make use of their weight, through studying the 'controlled fall'. Not only is a great deal of energy saved, but inner tension is also released, as the player has to breathe in when raising the arm and breathe out when dropping it, though he might not be aware of it.

It has been mentioned again and again that the shoulders must be dropped. This should be particularly watched with inexperienced players who find that their shoulders are forced upwards by the key reaction. Since any action causes a reaction, it is understandable that the key depression causes an upward reaction (in direct ratio with the energy used) — but this should be arrested at the knuckles, otherwise it causes undue tension all along the arms, right up to the neck and back of the player.

d) Face

C.P.E. Bach insists that the artist's face should express the mood of the piece performed. No one denies that the emotion of the artist should be communicated, but is it necessary to smile when playing a lively movement or put on a tragic, mournful expression when the music demands it?

We are concerned here with those exaggerated facial contortions and grimaces which are one more proof of the amount of unnecessary tension created in many parts of the body when only the involvement of a certain group of muscles would do. The same thing happens when a pianist sometimes plays a passage with one hand and the other contracts in sympathy.

Quite often, many fine players express the intensity of their emotion through some contractions of the face, and occasionally even great artists are heard groaning. This certainly brings them great relief, as much inner tension is eliminated through those heavy exhalations.

But, when the grimaces, mainly round the mouth and jaws, are caused by inability or too much anxiety, these have to be watched. A good idea is to place a mirror next to the music so that the student is forced to observe himself while practising. This usually makes him laugh, and has the right effect as there is no better way of releasing tension than laughter and good humour.

It is essential though that pianists and teachers should be aware of certain points which can become centres of accumulated tension. These are: *The wrists, the shoulders, the neck and back* and *the face.*

All through this essay we have been discussing various ways of coping with the tension which we continuously create. As regards these particular 'centres', it is a known fact that we can release tension in any part of the body by concentrating the attention on those areas that are tense points. But this mental exercise is not easily grasped, particularly by young pupils.

Exercises Here are some exercises, away from the instrument, combined with breathing, which should give the student a clear idea of the sensation of a tense and a loose organ.

1. *For wrists:*
    a) contract the fist — breathing in
    b) let go — breathing out
2. *For shoulders, neck and back:*
    a) raise both shoulders (as high as possible) — breathing in
    b) Let them drop — breathing out.

This is also one of the best exercises for learning the use of arm weight, the student becoming aware of the weight coming down in the hands.

At the same time every pianist — and for that matter, every performer should learn to attain the state of body balance through this mental exercise:

a) The pianist, in playing position, with hands placed on the keyboard, should direct his concentration to his head, trying to find its *point of balance* when it is "sitting" loosely on top of the spine. The player should experience the sensation of his head becoming weightless, with the spine gently pulled upwards.

b) A long exhalation, acting on the diaphragm, loosens the shoulders, back and neck, while the arms also hang loosely. The player should slowly oscillate the arms until they have become weightless and the upper part of the body feels so light as if it were not there.

c) At this point the pianist should direct his attention to his ankles, imagining them very loose. He should be aware of the most extraordinary sensation, that of his whole body becoming light, almost floating in space as if the force of gravity had lost its power.

d) All that is left — and this invariably happens — is to *smile*. Any residue of tension at the back of the neck miraculously disappears through this natural physical act.

In conclusion I should like to point out that I have tried to discuss as many facets as possible of this vast and mysterious problem in the hope that pianists and teachers may realize that tension is a healthy phenomenon and that we must be grateful for this immense gift with which nature has endowed us. Moreover, if we are to attain our goal — a balance between continuously generating tension and releasing it — we must also arrive at a complete, superb coordination between the body, the music and the instrument, namely a perfect fusion between the inner rhythm, the musical rhythm of the work performed, and the instrument.

It is through adopting a positive attitude that real progress can be achieved. This, in turn, will bring the realization that, while in the preparation of the performance, the player must study carefully the movements involved and consciously observe the freedom of breathing — during the performance he must trust his body. It will serve him faithfully if the state of balance is maintained and the harmonious muscular condition is there, unhindered, leaving the mind free to concentrate on the music to be interpreted and communicated to the listeners.

Now that *tension* is acknowledged as an integral part of our lives, we must face it, accept it and learn to cope with all its aspects and complexities.

The famous dictum: "To play the piano, one must hit the right key, with the right finger, at the right moment," could perhaps be thus paraphrased: "To play the piano efficiently one must have the right amount of tension, in the right place, at the right moment".

GERVASE DE PEYER

Clarinet Playing and the Control of Tension

There are two quite different activities involved in playing a wind instrument which can be considered separately. Firstly, as with singers, there is the process of tone production and how to sustain it, which is an internal bodily activity; secondly there is 'technique', which is the vocal or digital process of controlling the tone with all possible dexterity throughout the whole range of the instrument.

Indeed, one can say that the playing of wind instruments is a kind of singing: both demand the active usage of the diaphragm, chest, lungs, throat and facial musculature in producing the tone and controlling its volume and colour. However, the technique of wind instruments also involves the use of the fingers and the relevant muscles of the arms, shoulders, thorax and back to support the instrument and co-ordinate the necessary intricate controls. This whole process involves a subtle interplay of tension and relaxation.

Let us consider these two aspects separately and in depth.

One often observes performers inhibited by anxiety or the physical tension which affect the quality of their playing. Some singers seem to be wearing a steel corset, or, on the contrary, have jerky movements and faces which contort in grimaces. There are wind players who move their instrument around as if it were a baton or a flag communicating an hysterical semaphor. These

indicate tension in muscles that are not directly concerned with singing or playing and point to an inbalance
of tension in the use of necessary muscles. At the same
time the breathing process appears unatural and hampered through tensions which spread to other muscles
quite involuntarily. Great awareness is necessary for the
performer to analyze accurately how and where these
tensions occur.

Posture is of primary importance. The body must be
naturally erect and balanced so that the rib cage is
supported in an open position to allow the lungs to
expand freely when receiving air drawn in by use of the
all-important diaphragm. The diaphragm moves upwards
into the cavity of the rib cage, when air is expelled from
the lungs, through the instrument. Breathing in while
playing is achieved through openings between the lips
created momentarily, each side of the mouthpiece to
co-ordinate with the downwards push of the diaphragm.
This quick breathing demands no more than a 'flicking
smile' of the lip formation with no other tension than in
the muscles moving the diaphragm.

The muscular tension involved in supporting the rib-
cage in this way is minimal and passive, not complex
and active as it would be if this rib structure is used as
a bellows by continually expanding and contracting.
The player must practise long notes, exploring slowly
and smoothly a wide range of dynamics, controlled
absolutely by the diaphragm.

The focal point in tone production for a singer is the
vocal cords, whereas for a wind player it is the mouthpiece of the flute, the mouthpiece and reed of the clarinet,
or the reed alone in the case of the oboe and bassoon. It
is interesting to note that clarinet, oboe and bassoon
players have most of their mouthpiece and reed outside
the mouth while flute, like brass players, do not take
any part of the mouthpiece between their lips.

In playing wind instruments the musculature of the

face, throat and lips is used to control the quality of tone produced. This combination of muscles together with teeth, tongue and bone structure is called *embouchure*. A satisfactory tone production can only be achieved by the maximum relaxation of this embouchure. Tension, of course, exists particularly in the facial muscles which are in contact with the mouthpiece and reed but it is important that this is controlled and that a correct balance of tension and relaxation is maintained. Unnecessary clenching of the jaw, tightening of the neck and involuntary movement of the tongue should be avoided.

It is easily understandable how a correctly balanced state of these muscles can affect a singer's voice emanating from the vocal cords, since the throat, mouth and lips act as a complex resonator rather like a megaphone. It is more difficult to understand that these same factors are crucial in developing a clear, resonant tone in a wind instrument. As clarinet and other wind players have most of the reed and mouthpiece outside the mouth how can it be expected that the throat and the cavity within the mouth will have any obvious effect on tone production? The effect is nevertheless crucial and tension in this area can diminish and dull the tone.

As in singing, the capacity of the throat and mouth may 'help' the basic sound produced, in this case, by the vibrating reed. This is accomplished by allowing this 'chamber' to remain as open as possible without tension. Any rigidity will muffle the vibrations instead of augmenting them and any narrowing of this 'resonating chamber' will reduce the volume and richness of the tone by damping vital harmonics. To produce a fuller and richer tone, the palate and throat should be shaped as if speaking or singing the sound 'O' (as in 'ONLY') or 'AW' (as in 'CLAW') while breathing in a relaxed way from the diaphragm. The embouchure must be as relaxed as possible and the control of the reed should be accomplished with slight tension only at the 'tips of the lips'. In this way the player can control the reed, produce a clear tone and focus the resonance which has been set up by the mouth and throat cavity.

There is a parallel between the state of the rib cage while breathing and the correct shape of the mouth and throat cavities. The openness of this chamber allows the maximum resonance and is maintained without continuous muscular activity and the resulting variation of tensions. This is part of what I call *the correct support of the tone* together with the capacity for breathing produced by the properly supported rib cage when air is drawn into lungs through the use of the diaphragm. These 'holding tensions', once perfected, eliminate the interference of others which would obviously affect the performance.

The first part of this essay deals with the processes involved in the production of tone and how to sustain it, while the next part will discuss the activities referred to as 'technique', the vocal or digital process of controlling the tone. It is obvious that with such complex muscular interplay as is involved in mastering all the irregular finger patterns (which are more complicated on the clarinet than on other wind instruments), the minimum of tension will allow for greater dexterity. As all physical movements are the result of muscular activity, the correct 'balance' of tension and relaxation is the key to a good performance. Care must be taken that the stance of the player feels and looks comfortable and natural. The feet should be slightly apart, the body erect and at ease with the head poised, neither tilted forward nor backward. The instrument is brought up to the mouth at an angle of about 45° from the body and should point straight ahead of the player. The elbows are not forced into the waist and the wrists and hands are as much as possible a continuation of the forearm. The hands should not be at an angled position, or the wrists bent either up or down since this is bound to cause non-productive tension.

The playing of wind instruments involves certain relationships between *one's physical make-up* specifically the shape and size of the hands, the length and thickness of the fingers with their padded tips — and the fixed *lay-out or structure of the instruments*, with keys, levers with touchpiece, holes (with or without rings) that come to the player as a standard product of the instrument-maker. There is no doubt that since the development of the earliest instruments in the 17th century, manufacturers have always been concerned with this detailed lay-out, no matter what fingering system was being used (Boëhm, simple or others).

The result — it is hoped — is the best compromise between an ideal position of hand and fingers and the necessary positioning of holes to produce satisfactory intonation in any key. There is, of course, no such thing as a standard measurment of each finger in relation to the others and the length of the arms or indeed a standard ratio beteen arm length, size of hand and length of fingers. Therefore an instrument which, though quite comfortable for some to play, can give rise to strain in others and may need a marked degree of adjustment to suit an individual. Some clarinetists have found their own way by extending or shortening certain keys, usually those controlled by the little finger of each hand. Other areas sometimes need adjustments such as the position of the thumb rest, the point at which the right hand supports the instrument, at the same time maintaining a comfortable playing position; or the distance that the first finger of the left hand has to move to fulfill it diverse functions when using a Boëhm system clarinet, where it controls F sharp and B natural, by covering and uncovering the ringed tone hole and also connecting with or avoiding the throat tones, keys A and A flat. Both these areas are often centres of tensions and the more surely these problems are anticipated and dealt with the less likelihood that anxieties arising from physical inadequacy will inhibit the player.

It must be remembered that the first contact of many wind players with their instrument comes too late in their physical development having missed the opportunity for the necessary muscular and physical adjustments at an early age. On the other hand, it is physically impossible for a young player with a small hand to attain the necessary stretch and span between the fingers, particularly in the case of the clarinet, and the bassoon because the tone-holes have to be covered directly and sealed by the fleshy pad under the last phalanx of each finger; whereas the modern flute, oboe or saxophone has a built-in pad under a touchpiece which seals and closes the hole, which makes playing much easier. However the successful performer will be greatly helped by his ability to analyse and diagnose his individual problems correctly and solve them either by skilfully doing his own adjustments or discussing them with the instrument maker. These fundamentals are seldom mentioned and a young student may spend many years trying to adapt to an unecessarily awkward mechanical arrangement of his instrument. In this respect, wind players face different challenges from pianists, string players or percussionists as their instruments do not make such specific physical demands.

The balance between tension and relaxation is also crucial for the clarinetist when having to cope with the problem of closing and opening the seven tone-holes using the first three fingers of each hand and the left thumb. Faulty manipulation of these fingers results in leaks of air causing squeaks, poor intonation and a lack of clear articulation. Care must be taken to ensure that each finger covers its tone-hole with absolute precision. This means that the fleshy pad of the finger descends accurately and firmly over its tone-hole to achieve a perfect seal so that none of the moving air inside the clarinet can inadvertently escape through that particular tone-hole. When this happens a different note will be produced. To avoid this, the action of each finger must be incisive and in perfect co-ordination with the other fingers involved in producing a sequence of notes.

The player's basic position when holding the instrument depends on the grip of the fingers concerned with the seven holes. If this grip is too tight it can produce tension elsewhere in the hands with the consequent inhibition of elasticity and freedom of movement, particularly in the little fingers of each hand. Their task is to manipulate a variety of keys with touchpieces, which are grouped in such a way that they can be operated without disturbing the basic grip on the tone-holes. This may become a major cause of tension since anxiety about proper coverage of these tone-holes is common to performers and it often produces psychological tensions which in themselves lead to other physical problems. Which one of us has not experienced increased difficulties when attempting to repeat a passage where we have previously failed? This can teach us that our mental approach to playing must remain fresh, optimistic and relaxed; qualities born of the knowledge that we understand our problems and how to cope with them. This surely is the only path to success.

The most common bad habit resulting from anxiety is using too much energy in activating each finger and then maintaining too much pressure to ensure that the hole remains covered. To remedy this the player must consciously relax each finger so that only the minimal effort is used to ensure proper coverage of each hole after the initial impact. This instant relaxation is absolutely necessary, and possibly still more important is the maintenance of a relaxed position of the hands when the fingers are not in use. The best position is when the fingers are poised over the tone-holes just high enough to allow the free passage of air through them from inside the 'tube' without affecting the intonation by inhibiting this air-flow in any way. The extent to which each finger has to bend to achieve this depends on the size of the hand and length of the fingers. However, if the fingers are too straight or too bent difficulties might result through tension caused by this awkward position. The best way is to relate the grip on the instrument to the manner in which one would hold something, such as a ball, a handle, a tennis racket or a steering wheel.

In the hurly-burly of our hectic lives it is such a waste of time and energy to have to cope with unnecessary problems and difficulties. We all have, and always will have, high standards if we are genuine artists and living up to their demands in our attempts to do justice to great music requires discipline as well as inspiration. Too often, though, our work may be hampered by factors that we do not properly understand or that we do not realize that we can control. When too much relaxation and of the wrong sort occurs, the result is dull and boring music-making. There is no doubt that vigilance and awareness can help us avoid tensions of all kinds. But to succeed we must beware of the possible danger of allowing our performance to lose edge, vitality and immediacy. It is also true that the more deeply an artist is involved and affected emotionally by the music he or she performs, the more difficult it becomes to keep a cool control or the supremely subtle organisation that is behind each performance.

Cool head but hot fingers could be the motto, but even that is not completely true since the head sometimes needs to produce heat while the fingers certainly need to remain cool.

PAUL LEHRER

Performance Anxiety and How to Control it:
A Psychologist's Perspective

Anxiety is part of the life of all human beings, but performing artists suffer more than their fair share of it. Many anxiety-producing factors converge to make performance one of the more stressful occupations: the competitiveness of the field, the desire to give a "perfect" performance, being under close critical observation by audience and critics, and the need to have complete control over the very psychobiological processes that are most impaired by anxiety (muscular coordination, concentration, and memory). In this chapter I will review some of the psychological research and theory on anxiety, and discuss how this helps us to understand performance anxiety and gives us some tools to manage it.

Psychological research on anxiety has shown anxiety to have three components: (1) A physiological component (rapid heart beat, sweating and the other forms of physiological arousal with which most musicians are familiar); (2) a cognitive component (worrying about unpleasant things happening, inability to think clearly); and (3) a behavioral component (not doing some things that one ordinarily would do, avoiding doing or thinking things that would provoke anxiety). These three components of anxiety are not very well correlated with each other. Sometimes we experience one of these components, sometimes another; and sometimes we experience all three together. Similarly, my research and clinical experience suggests that each of these kinds of anxiety symptoms responds best to a different form of treatment.

Physiological Symptoms and Their Control (A) *

Phylogenetically, our bodies are not designed to face the rigors of concert performance. Rather, they are designed for survival in the jungle: for finding food and shelter, for maintaining body warmth, for reproduction, and for coping with life threatening situations (e.g. being chased by bears). The last of these evokes what has come to be termed the "flight or fight reaction." Under stress, our bodies are designed for fighting or for getting away. Those of our ancestors who couldn't do these things very effectively died, so we no longer have their traits.

From the point of view of natural adaptation, there are certain things that should happen when we are really in an emergency situation.

(1) We must increase our mental alertness, and think fast. One of the most adaptive of all human traits, and the one that differentiates us from all other animals, is the capability for complex thought. In emergencies, we think better and faster, and thus avoid or cope with danger.

(2) Another important trait in emergencies is agility, speed, and strength. Under stress people can be capable of extraordinary physical feats: e.g. a frail mother lifting an automobile to get her child out from under it. Also our tactile senses become sharpened, and we are better able to do things, this being partly the result from increased sweating in the palms and the soles of the feet. Sweating in the palms and soles is *not* part of the body's temperature regulation system — as is sweating from the back, chest, or forehead. Rather this form of sweat *only* occurs during psychological alertness, and its function is to increase agility. This has implications for music performance. Most instrumentalists find it rather difficult to play when their hands too dry!

are too dry. The hands slip and have less ability to 'hold on.' On the other hand, too much moisture, as may occur in states of high anxiety, also makes playing difficult. This amount of moisture is more adaptive for climbing rocks and trees, for running over rough terrain without shoes, etc., than it is for playing musical instruments.

3. Finally, the body must protect itself from damage. Two ways in which it does this are peripheral vasoconstriction and increased muscle tension.

Peripheral vasoconstriction. When we become anxious, the blood vessels on the surface of the body – particularly in the hands and feet – constrict. This causes sensations of cold hands and feet, because there is less blood circulating in these areas. Thus, if we get injured there is less blood near the outside of the body, and hence more protection against blood loss. Peripheral vasoconstriction also occurs when the temperature is too cold. This is part of the body's way of regulating its own internal temperature. It keeps the blood from being cooled by the outside air, and keeps the vital organs warm. Peripheral vasoconstriction also allows more blood to flow the the large muscles of the body. This is adaptive for fight or flight. It provides nourishment to the big muscles in order to prepare for running away or fighting. However, cold hands do decrease tactile sensitivity and fine muscle coordination in the extremeties, and this can affect instrumental performance.

Increased muscle tension. The most noticeable physiological effect of the fight or flight reaction often is muscular tension throughout the body. This protects the body from injury caused by being struck, and may enhance physical strength. However, it can be disastrous for musicians. Each movement we make requires tension in the active muscle and *relaxation* in the 'opposing' muscles, i.e., the muscles that would make us perform the opposite motion. When all the muscles tense at once we feel muscle bound and are not able to perform well in tasks requiring complex fine motor skills.

Optimum Level of Physiological Arousal

Is anxiety necessarily something to be avoided all the time? Chronic anxiety and chronic tension are obviously not healthy. They can lead to psychosomatic disorders, and can impair day-to-day functioning. However, at times, a certain amount of physiological arousal is helpful. Many laboratory studies have found an inverted "U" function between the amount of anxiety or arousal and the ability to perform a variety of tasks. This function is the closest thing that psychologists have found to a 'law' of behaviour, analogous to the laws of thermodynamics in physics. We call it the Yerkes Dodson Law, named after two psychologists who first described the function. Yerkes and Dodson found that performance on a moderately difficult task is facilitated by a moderate amount of anxiety or physiological arousal. If arousal is too low or too high, performance is impaired: hence the inverted 'U'. On the other hand, very difficult taks are performed best with very low arousal, and very simple tasks under very high arousal. Concert performance, presumably, is a moderately difficult task. This may seem surprising upon first reading. Certainly the skills involved in concert performance are very difficult. However, they must not be difficult for the performer at the time of the performance. Ordinarily the performer is not thinking out strategies, musical concepts or physical coordination during the performance. This has already been done during preparation for the concert (a time when very low anxiety would presumably be most adaptive).

Techniques for Treating the Physiological Components of Anxiety

The most commonly used modern technique for treating

the physiological components of anxiety is taking tranquilizers. Tranquilizers are by far the most commonly prescribed of all drugs. However, tranquilizing medication is difficult to regulate and it often has undersirable side effects. Often it takes *too* much anxiety away, so that the performer no longer 'cares' enough to give a good performance. Alternatively, it may not be strong enough to block a panic attack. Also, if taken regularly, most tranquilizing medication is addictive, physically as well as psychologically. As we become less able to predict and control our emotions without the use of drugs, we become increasingly more anxious and more drug dependent.[1] For these reasons, I encourage people to avoid taking tranquilizers on a regular basis.

The quieting response. The American psychiatrist, Charles Stroebel, has described an almost ludicrously simple technique designed to help people to manage mild everyday anxiety. When you begin to feel tension building up, do the following: (1) Smile, (2) Take two very slow very deep breaths, and (3) Tell yourself, "Keep my body out of this." The smile is included because it changes patterns of facial muscle tension that habitually occur during anxiety. Facial muscle tension appears to be quite different for various emotional states, and changing the pattern of facial muscle tension appears to have some effect in actually changing the emotions that people feel. The deep breaths have direct effects on the cardiovascular system, and can produce a temporarily somewhat lower state of

---

[1] Recently some research has been done on a drug called Propranolol, which blocks many of the physiological effects of anxiety apparently without adversely affecting physical agility or mental processes. We must await long-term evaluation of the effects of this drug before recommending its use. Propranolol is known to be medically dangerous to some individuals, and its propensity to produce psychological addiction is not known.

physiological arousal. Telling yourself to "Keep my body out of this" helps to put the situation in better perspective. Below I will explain more about such "cognitive" strategies for reducing anxiety.

Eastern self-regulatory disciplines. Over the centuries Eastern cultures have laid relatively greater importance than have Western cultures on the subjective experience of inner calm. These cultures have developed a number of techniques, attitudes, and disciplines that are designed to help people to achieve that end. Thus practitioners of yoga, tai chi, aikido, and various Eastern forms of meditation all are trained to regulate the tension they experience in their minds and bodies. Laboratory studies of some yogis and tai chi masters have verified that these people have developed remarkable control over the nervous system, including the parts of the nervous system that regulate cardiovascular and other vegetative functions. Although study of these disciplines would probably be helpful to the performing musician, the time and the dedication that they require in order to attain such mastery are often unacceptable to Westerners, as are some of the philosophical, religious, and metaphysical assumptions that accompany the disciplines. Thus several Western approaches have been developed which are more acceptable to our culture, if not more 'efficient' in producing the desired effects. Some of these will be described below.

The Alexander technique. This technique was devised by an actor who had experienced tension symptons that prevented him from continuing to act. It involves learing to assume and to cultivate a bodily posture that promotes relaxation. Although very little scientific research has been done on the effects of the Alexander technique, its widespread long-term use suggests that it does have beneficial effects. There is some laboratory evidence suggesting that, when a person learns to hold the body in a relaxed posture after training in this technique, muscular tension is, in fact, reduced.

iv b

Progressive relaxation. A muscular relaxation technique that has been subject to widespread research and clinical use is Edmund Jacobson's technique of progressive relaxation. Usually we are unaware of the constant activity in our muscles throughout the body. Progressive relaxation involves learning how to recognize this activity — including the very *low* amounts of muscle tension involved in everyday muscle tone — and learning how to 'switch it off' and how to stop *doing* things. The effects of progressive relaxation go far beyond the muscular system. Approximately 70% of the sensory input to the brain comes from sensory receptors within the muscles that carry information about muscle tension. Thus if the muscles are all completely relaxed, the brain also tends to 'relax', and to quiet the thought processes and vegetative activity that usually accompany tension. This technique is widely used to treat anxiety, phobias, and various psychosomatic symptoms, including certain forms of insomnia, headaches, hypertension, and gastro-intestinal and sexual problems.

iv c

Autogenic training. Another Western technique of self-regulation is autogenic training, a technique derived by Johannes Schultz, a German physician who worked at the turn of the century. Schultz studied the various effects of hypnosis, and noticed that under hypnosis, many people experienced physiological sensations indicative of profound relaxation. These include heaviness and warmth in the limbs, warmth in the solar plexus, coolness in the forehead, a sensation of breathing automatically, and a feeling that the heart is beating more slowly. Autogenic training begins with six standard exercises, in which, through a procedure similar to self hypnosis, a person learns to achieve these feelings. The procedures involve 'passive concentration' on a series of 'autogenic formulas.' The formulas include, "My arms and legs are warm and heavy;" "My solar plexus is warm;" "My heartbeat is calm and regular." A person concentrating passively on these formulas will say them silently and may imagine the physical sensations involved, but must not *try* to achieve these sensations, because the very act of trying prevents the sensations occurring.

There has been much worldwide research on the effects of autogenic training. Like progressive relaxation, it has been found to be an effective treatment for anxiety and for a number of psychosomatic disorders. It appears to have its greatest effects on the vegetative functions, although it can also have profound effects on thought processes. An advanced practitioner can use it to help assume some of the more functional and less self-defeating mental attitudes that I shall discuss below. Its most immediate use for the instrumental performer may be for hand warming.

Biofeedback. The quintessentially Western approach to tension control is biofeedback. This approach uses electronic equipment and paramedical technicians to teach people to relax. Biofeedback can be used to help people to control any of a number of physiological functions, including muscle tension, heart rate and blood pressure, palmar and finger sweating, blood flow to the extremeties, and electroencephalographic (brain wave) rhythms. When a person undergoes biofeedback therapy, electrodes are attached to the sites at which measurements are being taken, and the signals taken from the recording sites are then amplified, often to hundreds of thousands of times their original amplitude. The amplified signal is then used to tell the person how much activity is being emitted by the physiological system being measured. This information may be in the form of a simple light, tone, or dial or, in laboratores endowed with computers. it may take the form of an elaborate graph, with 'target' levels at which subjects 'aim'.

Biofeedback has been demonstrated to help people

to control migraine and tension headaches, moderately high labile blood pressure, and Raynaud's disease. (The last of these is a disorder that severely limits or stops blood flow to the extremities in cold weather or during states of emotional tension. This disorder is often hereditary, but it can also be brought on by trauma to the fingers, which can be caused by frequent percussion or vibration. Its sympoms are unusually common among pianists.)

In one famous case, biofeedback was used to treat constriction of the throat muscles in a bassoon player. This constriction prevented the musician from playing. Muscle tension was measured via an electromyogram, through electrodes that were pasted to the person's neck. With biofeedback, the person learned to relax his vocal apparatus, and eventually he was able to resume playing the bassoon. Other more experimental applications of biofeedback include control of cardiac arrhythmias, epilepsy, postural disorders, encopresis (inability to retain feces) and chronic back pain. It is too early to tell whether the initial apparent successes of biofeedback with these latter problems will hold up under widespread clinical use and scientific scrutiny.

A major drawback to biofeedback is that it is usually inconvenient to give feedback to more than one or two physiological measures at a time, and relaxation skills learned in one physiological system often do not generalize to others. Also the feedback is often not available when it is needed the most (e.g. during or immediately before a concert performance). Thus when it is used to help people control high levels of general tension, it is most often applied in conjunction with one of the other relaxation techniques described in this chapter.

Cognitive Symptoms and Their Control

A cognition is a thought, and cognitions are the media

through which we understand the world. The American psychologist, George Kelly, has argued that we are incapable of knowning 'reality' directly. Rather, we 'construe' it through our cognitions about it. Often our cognitions about the world are highly idiosynchratic. Thus one person may think of a situation as being highly dangerous or ego-threatening, while another may think of the same situation as being safe or even humdrum. Another American psychologist, Richard Lazarus, has described the process through which cognitions may produce anxiety. The first part of the process involves perception of threat. When we perceive a possible danger in the environment we react immediately with anxiety. However, after evaluating a situation as stressful we start to look for ways to cope with the threat. When we convince ourselves that we can cope, the anxiety diminishes. Lazarus has described two types of coping processes: (1) Actually manipulating the environment so that the threat is neutralized; and (2) redefining the environment as less threatening than originally perceived. Both of these strategies have their place, and both can be cultivated by the performing artist. When neither is effectively used, the person may give way to panic.

First, let us catalog some of the situations that performing artists may perceive initially as threats: slips; muscle weakness or tension; inability to master some of the technical problems presented in the program; inattentiveness in the audience; ridicule by critics and/ or colleagues; the possibility of developing a bad public reputation or of losing the affection of friends and supporters who once were attracted to one partly because of one's performance talents; not understanding a piece of music sufficiently for one's own standards; unreliability of an instrument; strangeness of a new instrument or concert hall; and problems in living, financial, and travel arrangements associated with a concert tour. Also interpersonal worries, either personal or professional, can produce a chronically high level of anxiety that can sensitize one to all these other worries, and can amplify the symptoms of anxiety.

One tendency of people who do panic under certain kinds of stress is that they do not think enough about the threatening situation, and do not prepare themselves to cope with it. This was clearly demonstrated in a psychological study of parachute jumpers done by Seymour Epstein and Walter Fenz. Experienced parachute jumpers, who usually experience little anxiety at the time of a jump, experience a lot of anxiety in anticipation of the jump. This anticipatory anxiety is measureable as much as a week or more before the jump. Novice parachute jumpers, on the other hand, show relatively little anxiety in the days before the jump, but have tremendous increases in anxiety *immediately* before the jump, and often panic at the time of the jump. One possible explanation for these findings is that the experienced parachute jumpers are cognitively preparing themselves for the jump during their period of anticipatory anxiety. They are thinking of all the possible things that could go wrong with them or their equipment, and are developing strategies for coping with these things or, alternatively, they are "coming to terms" with the possibility of disaster and the ultimate inevitability of death but, at the time of the jump, have decided that the risk is worthwhile and much less threatening. *Thus worrying about things in advance may help reduce anxiety about them when they occur.* I have spoken to a number of performers who deliberately rehearse the concert situation in their minds for weeks before the concert, and deliberately think out their feelings about all the possible things that could go wrong, and mentally rehearse strategies for coping. They then report that, at the concert, they experience much less anxiety. This procedure is similar to a treatment technique called 'desensitization' that is used by many mental health practitioners to treat phobias. I have successfully used it to help several people with performance anxiety. In this technique the person designs a 'hierarcy' of related fears, ranging from those that evoke very little anxiety to those which evoke panic. Then, using one of the relaxation procedures above, the person relaxes and begins imagining the hierarchy item that evokes the *least* anxiety. When imagining this item no longer evokes anxiety, the person advances to the next most anxiety-producing item. This goes on until the person is able to imagine the most anxiety-producing item without experiencing any anxiety. The original rationale for this method is that anxiety responses are 'deconditioned' through a process similar to that employed by Pavlov in his famous experiments on salivation in dogs. However, there is some strong clinical evidence that this method also works by helping people to change their cognitions about the feared situation. While the person is imagining the anxiety-provoking situations (s)he is also thinking about how to cope with them.

The most important coping technique for a performing artist, obviously, is to have properly rehearsed the music, understood it, and solved all the technical problems involved in the performance. No psychological technique can substitute for proper artistic preparation. This should include preparation for some predictable contingencies: e.g., a memory slip or feelings of muscle tightness. Preparation of the music should include strategies for gracefully finding one's place when one is lost, and for relaxing muscles that have, because of any anxiety and/or technical problems, become tight. The music itself should present no technical and no conceptual surprises to the artist during the performance — although the heightened physiological and mental arousal produced by the performance situation may make the performer more alert to some nuances that were previously missed, thus producing the 'electricity' in many live performances that are often missing in recordings made in sound studies.

Similarly the artist should have thought about strategies for solving some of the nonmusical problems that go along with a concert tour: interpersonal encounters, financial and travel arrangements, etc. The natural tendency to put off thinking about stressful, or unpleasant, or seemingly unsolvable problems can produce a greater anxiety at performance time. Setting some time aside for 'constructive worrying' weeks before a performance can help in developing coping skills.

In contrast to this, some individuals appear to worry too much in advance, and to paralyze themselves. Actually, however, it is usually not the amount of worrying that is usually excessive, but the form it takes: negative self-statements, catastrophizing, and seemingly uncontrollable "intrusive" thoughts that interfere with organized thought and functioning.

Negative self-thoughts. One characteristic of individuals who suffer from incapacitating performance anxiety is the tendency to engage in negative thoughts about themselves. They tell themselves that they are not as good as other people in the field, that they do not have the intellectual or technical capability to master the music they are playing, and that they are generally unworthy and unlovable as human beings. This is often related to highly perfectionistic standards. There is often an implicit assumption that the next performance must be the definitive performance, and must be as 'good' as the performance of some other artist.

In my clinical practice I may ask people to rehearse some positive self-thoughts: e.g., "If I take one step at a time I can continue to improve my performance; I am performing in order to give pleasure to myself and others, not in order to meet *their* neurotic perfectionistic standards; no performance is ever perfect, but represents only my present stage in a life-long growth process; although I want this performance to be as good as it can be at this stage in my life, I know that there will be more performances later at which I can further improve; my personality and my skills are unique and valuable to me and I am not ashamed of them." The act of mouthing to oneself positive statements can make them appear to be more true.

Catastrophizing At times we all, in our minds, tend to make bad situations into catastrophes. Albert Ellis, a well known "cognitive therapist," has called this tendency "catastrophizing." The artist may tell him/herself that one mistake, or even one bad concert, will mean the end of a career; that it will make others ashamed and less loving; that it will cause public criticism; that anxiety will get out of control and make him/her appear ridiculous in public, etc. In fact, all of these unpleasant things actually *might* happen, and do happen on occasion. These are usually the *worst* things that may happen to an artist; but are they, in fact, catastrophes? People do survive them, learn from them, and prosper despite them. These things would be catastrophes only if they impaired our very survivial, or made us into truly unworthy or unlovable human beings; but they do not do these things. Anxiety is a human emotion that we all experience. The world does not come to an end when others realize that we are nervous. President Roosevelt told Americans during the Great Depression that "there is nothing to fear but fear itself." But even fear is no catastrophic. Similarly the greatest of artists have all survived bad reviews and public ridicule at some times in their lives. In fact, it is impossible to have *everyone* approve of us and of what we are doing. Criticism, even public criticism, is not catastrophic. We can learn from it or reject it as we see fit, but we still remain worthwhile as people. The fair weather friends who would reject us when we fail are not worth worrying

over, and their disapproval certainly should not affect
our own self image. If this attitude is held by a spouse, a
parent, or another individual on whom one actually is
dependent in some sense, appropriate assertive behaviour
should be directed toward them, because *they* are being
unfair. Finally, and most importantly, although a bad
performance may adversely affect one's career, at least
in the short run, even this need not be a catastrophe.
Seeking another form of livelihood is always possible,
and music can always be enjoyed on a nonpaying basis,
sometimes even more so than as a professional musician.
No one can take away the enjoyment that music has
brought, and professional comebacks are always possible.
Such an outcome might be jarring and unpleasant,
but is not catastrophic.

Treatment for catastrophizing usually involves
thinking rationally about one's catastrophic thoughts.
Usually these thoughts are irrational. There are few genuine catastrophes in this world. Exaggerating the genuine
risks of everyday life is nonproductive. One way to
engage in this type of rational thought is to think of all
the logical implications of our fearful thoughts, and to
perform *reductio ad absurdum.* Is it *really* the end of
the world if I get nervous on stage and everyone finds
out? Just imagine everyone in the audience gloating over
my misfortune, and abandoning me to isolation and
starvation. If the absurdity of this scenario is not
immediately self evident, then think of the experience
of survivors of genuine catastrophes: air crashes, fires,
floods, wars, death camps, etc. Even there, with survival
there is always hope. In music performance, survival is
not an issue.

Intrusive thoughts. Catastrophic thoughts, unpleasant
images, and negative self-thoughts can intrude into
consciousness at the most inopportune times. People
suffering from performance anxiety most often
experience these thoughts while they are trying to

practice, to organize plans for their concert tours, or to sleep. Often they prevent the very kind of systematic artistic preparation that will lower anxiety during the performance itself. When this happens, I suggest that the thoughts be treated simply as bad habits. Treatment of such habits involves several steps: (1) Observe what is happening each time you begin having these thoughts. What are you thinking about? Have you just started working on a difficult passage that has triggered these thoughts? Have you just had an interpersonal encounter that has reinforced negative self-thinking? Identifying these antecedents of the intrusive thoughts can help in pinpointing the particular irrational assumptions that are triggering the anxiety. (2) Count the thoughts. This will tell you how well you are doing in getting rid of them. Progress is usually gradual, and often is unnoticeable unless some careful records are kept. Also the very process of keeping records can reduce the frequency of the thoughts. Often it 'objectifies' the thoughts, and allows one to examine them critically. When the thoughts are no longer automatically accepted as 'reality' they can more easily be disposed of. (3) If all else fails, schedule some 'obsessional thinking' time, and deliberately think the catastrophic thoughts before facing situations, such as practice times, when the thoughts tend to occur naturally. Such 'negative practice' helps develop control over the thoughts. Thus, if you can turn the thoughts on, you can also turn them off. Also one can become tired of thinking them. Also, thinking the thoughts 'on schedule' prevents these thoughts from serving other functions, e.g., helping us to avoid facing difficult technical, or conceptual, or personal problems. Thus isolated from the personality functions that they play, the thoughts simply become boring, and thus are more easily cast aside.

Cognitive effects of meditation. Some simple *mantra* — meditation techniques, such as those popularized through the Transcendental Meditation movement, appear to have direct effects on the cognitive symptoms of anxiety, particularly the occurence of intrusive thoughts. Although various *mantras* have very specific meanings in Indian tradition, Western research has found that the specific *mantra* that is used makes very little difference. Choose any word that has soothing sounds, and whose meaning is totally unknown to you. In order to prevent it from developing unpleasant 'meanings,' do not tell it to anyone, and use it only during meditation.

Meditation may consist of time periods varying between a few minutes and a half hour or more. During this time be sure that there are no interruptions. Lock the door, and take the telephone off the hook. Others in the household must respect one's meditation time, and not intrude, except in emergencies. Sit so as to be looking at a pretty scene, painting, or flower arrangement. Then, close your eyes and repeat the *mantra* at any pace that seems comfortable to you at the time. If the *mantra* disappears for periods of time, that is fine, but if any uncomfortable thoughts arise try to return to the *mantra* directly. This method is spelled out in more detail in Patricia Carrington's recent book, *Freedom in Meditation.*

Meditation appears to have a particularly strong effect on worrying because it utilizes the same brain pathways that are used during worrying: the pathways involved in forming words. It is virtually impossible to think two words simultaneously. Thus the *mantra* can directly block worrying. Also, because meditation is almost invariably a pleasant experience, the *mantra* begins to develop pleasant associations, and eventually elicits pleasant thoughts and images. It can become a powerful tool in combatting catastrophic and negative thoughts and images.

Behavioral Symptoms of Anxiety and Their Control

The major behavioral effect of anxiety is that it makes us avoid doing things. Very severely anxious people may become "agoraphobic," i.e., they may stay at home all the time and be afraid to go anyplace because going places creates anxiety. Certainly, as described above, anxiety can make one avoid thinking about the concert that will occur a few weeks hence. It can also prevent one from thinking about analyzing the passages in the music that are difficult to learn. I recently spoke with one music teacher who teaches his students to isolate and to concentrate on such passages. People have a natural tendency to spend time mainly with the parts that they are able to play well, because these create less anxiety.

Another important behaviorally oriented anxiety-reduction technique is simply to perform very frequently. The 'incubation effect' is a well-known phenomenon in psychology. The longer one stays away from a threatening situation, the greater the anxiety that occurs when one is again faced with it. Folklore tells us that, when thrown by a horse we should immediately get back on, or we may never ride again. Similarly for musical performance. A bad review or an unsuccessful concert should not be taken as a reason to stop performing. Although many artists have found that periods away from the stage can be good times for rethinking their technique and their understanding of music, this is often done at the risk of increases in performance anxiety when concertizing is resumed. At times it may be well worth this risk, but the reality of this risk should be considered when the decision is made.

What To Do When Anxiety Is Too High
In this chapter I have described some psychological theories of anxiety, and I have described some techniques for combatting it in musical performance. These techniques will not completely eliminate anxiety. Such

an effect would be impossible as well as undersirable. Some anxiety makes musical performance, as well as life itself, more interesting. There is now an increasing proliferation of 'self-help' books that describe in more detail many of the techniques I have mentioned here. More serious problems with anxiety may not respond at all to the self-help approach, because the anxiety may prevent us from thinking clearly about the sources of the anxiety and the proper strategies for overcoming it. As other chapters in this book demonstrate, music educators are developing interests in helping people systematically to manage anxiety and tension and, if that fails, there is still the psychotherapist. Although anxiety will always be with us, it need not always be a source of fear.

EDMUND JACOBSON M.D.

A Manual
of
Tension Control

Introduction by Paul Lehrer

Below is a reprint of one of the classic relaxation training manuals. It was written by Edmund Jacobson, the psychologist and physician who first studied the principles of relaxation in the scientific laboratory and applied them to the treatment of various psychological and somatic ills. The manual contains a series of instructions aimed at teaching you to become more aware of even the very tiniest amounts of tension in the muscles, and to develop the ability to eliminate muscle tension at will. It contains instructions that must be practised regularly. The discipline involved is painstaking and time-consuming, but the results are rewarding.

At the outset, let me pose and answer some questions that the reader may naturally ask at this point. What are the rewards of obtaining relaxation skills, and could they possibly justify adding an hour of relaxation practice to an already overly busy daily schedule? Why should a technique that focuses entirely on muscle relaxation (vs., say, mental relaxation) be useful in reducing performance stress? What is the value of relaxation to the performing artist? Is it not possible that too much relaxation will harm performance more than help it?

The rewards of having relaxation skills. Everyone experiences the ill effects of stress at some point in life. The adverse physical and mental effects are legion. Medical research has found that stress can be a contributing factor to a variety of illnesses, including heart disease, stroke, cancer, and various infectious diseases. Everyone also experiences situations in which control of anxiety or rage could improve personal adaptiveness, problem-solving, and understanding.

Performers, however, may experience the effects of stress even more keenly than others. The performance situation requires a level of mental and physical functioning and control that lies at the outer limits of human ability. Slight impairments can produce major effects on quality of performance. Although an optimal degree of "facilitating" anxiety may improve performance to a point, the keen competition and perfectionistic demands of the performer's world can easily tip the balance in the deleterious direction. All performers have experienced deleterious effects of tension at some performances or auditions. Therefore learning the skills to modulate this tension might be as useful as learning other subtle aspects of instrumental technique. All of music performance involves the application of exquisite physical and mental self-control to the production of music. Relaxation can help to maximize this control, particularly under conditions of physical and emotional stress.

Why muscular relaxation? As I have outlined previously in this volume, there are many approaches to relaxation and stress control. Some emphasize various aspects of mental control, and others various kinds of physical control. I have chosen to present a detailed description of a muscular approach for two reasons: (1) Emotional arousal may combine with technical problems at the instrument and produce isometric muscle tension (i.e., a state in which opposing muscles tense simultaneously, and prevent each other from performing their tasks of moving parts of the body). Because of the demands for peak muscular coordination and control in most forms of musical performance, excess muscle tension can be particularly troublesome for the performing artist. Muscle relaxation skills therefore are especially relevant for controlling the particular tension problems that are most often faced by the performer.

In addition, learning muscular control does generalize to other areas of functioning. When stress speeds up mental processes to the point of confusion, physical relaxation skills can be used to slow it down to an optimal level. Similarly muscular relaxation can produce a number of indirect physical effects that are particularly beneficial for performers. These include warming and drying the hands and fingers, and moistening the throat. Although undoubtedly some musicians will find such techniques as autogenic training or mantra meditation to be more helpful and/or more enjoyable to do, I have chosen to present a detailed description of muscle relaxation here because I would expect it to have the most immediately beneficial effects for the widest number of performers. Also, other than for the considerable time and discipline it entails, most people find it to be enjoyable. If, however, you happen to find that this technique goes against your grain, or if you feel that another technique might better meet your needs, by all means try that one first! Although the effects of the various relaxation techniques do differ in subtle ways, no one of them has proven to be generally superior to any other; and you will find yourself better able and willing to use a technique that "fits" you than one that does not.

or choose another [margin note]

A3 *Can relaxation be harmful to performance?* Musicians often ask whether relaxation can be harmful to performance, because, they feel that they must be sufficiently "keyed up" to give an effective performance. There is, in fact, some research evidence that this concern is justified. Relaxation is not a religion (although meditative relaxation techniques do play some part in most religions). As presented here, it is a technique that is powerful in controlling maladaptive tension levels.

Elsewhere in this volume I have described the "Yerkes-Dodson" law in psychology, which predicts that a *moderate* degree of anxiety should be optimal for performance. If anxiety levels are too high *or too low* performance suffers. Presumably, then, relaxation techniques should be used when you feel too anxious or tense, or even too muscle-bound because of technical difficulties at the instrument. The technique should not be used when you feel blasé about a particular performance and when your level of comfort and control at the instrument already are at optimal levels.

NB caution [margin note]

A4 *How to use this manual.* The time you spend practising the techniques described in this manual is analogous to the time you spend practising your instrument. The time is spent learning and practising a skill. In order for this skill to be of use to you, you must *use* it when you need to. Here are two suggestions for doing so:

(1) If you feel that a performance will be particularly stressful for you, spend a few minutes relaxing immediately before it. Remember, this may not have very profound effects when you first start learning the progressive relaxation technique. Like

all complex muscular skills, the skill of relaxation takes time to develop.

2) If maladaptive tension develops in the middle of a performance, make deliberate use of the relaxation technique in order to eliminate the tension while performing. After a while, relaxing muscles becomes almost automatic, requiring very little conscious attention. You can learn to relax un-needed muscles, while using other muscles in order to perform, without diminishing your ability to concentrate on the music. This use of the technique is called "differential relaxation". Differential relaxation can be used to diminish the excessive isometric tension that often can get in the way of performance. It is by far the most difficult aspect of the progressive relaxation technique; and, for some applications, personal instruction may be necessary, carried out by a teacher or coach who is familiar with the principles of relaxed instrumental playing.

Self-Operations Control

INTRODUCTION

Tension Symptoms and Complaints
Two Faces of the Same Coin

Your tension symptoms are sufficient indication that you do not know how to run your organism efficiently. However, you can learn to do this, just as you can learn to run a car. Once you have learned, you will not have to keep your mind on your muscles any more than when you walk. Control becomes a habit, second nature, and occurs almost automatically as a better way of living.

Tension symptoms in you, as in others, may include undue fatigue, poor sleep, irritability, constipation, spells of diarrhea following strain, abdominal pains, palpitation, tight feelings in the chest, poor concentration, dizziness, weakness and an extensive variety of pains and discomforts.

Do not watch symptoms. Develop skill as you would in learning to swim or to play some game. Just see what happens as you learn to save your energies! Signs of progress may appear soon, even within a few days; or there may be delay, depending upon your state and other matters. But if you practice daily, you are doing something that is basic!

Running Your Car

To run your car, you sit in the driver's seat and manipulate the ignition key, the accelerator, the gear shift or hydromatic drive, the steering wheel and the brake. These are the controls. See Figure 1 on page 2.

By manipulating the controls, you make the wheels go around at a rate and in the direction which suit your purposes. This is driving.

You yourself are a living instrument which can be run like your car, if you know how. You will be the driver, for nobody else can do it.

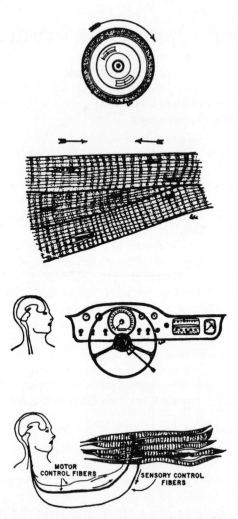

Fig. 1. You run your car by manipulating the controls on and near the dashboard, whereby you make the wheels move at the rate and in the direction you desire. Likewise, you can run yourself by going on and off with the power in the controls which lie in your muscles, whereupon your muscles contract and relax in the patterns which suit your effort-purposes.

You have no wheels, but you have the equivalent. Muscles are the equivalent. Wheels turn and can do so because they are made of hard, brittle materials. Muscles are plastic and soft, and thus they can perform in many ways far better than wheels.

Everything you do from morning till night and from night till morning is done by muscles. What muscles look like is familiar to you. Raw steak is muscle.

Muscles are made up of fibers. Each fiber is so thin that by itself it is invisible to the naked eye. Each one courses straight or round about. When fibers shorten, this is muscle contraction. You know it as "effort." When fibers lengthen, effort is discontinued. This is relaxation in the scientific sense of the word, which we shall use exclusively.

Every effort you make, then, is performed by shortening and ended by lengthening of muscle fibers.

When you think, you are making efforts, but you do not realize this. You are to learn to recognize these efforts. They include very complicated patterns of muscle tension and relaxation. Repeated practice helps, for tension signals are very slight and fleeting. You will learn to recognize them just as a telegrapher learns to recognize the sound signals of the Morse code.

What about your brain and nerves? There is no moving fiber in brain or nerves. Therefore they do not move you as wheels move the car. Certainly, your brain and nerves participate in your every effort, but they correspond, not to the wheels of your car, but to what lies under the hood. Brain and nerves are indispensable, for a child born without a brain could not move but would lie like a heap of flesh on the floor. However, your brain and your nerves are like telephone wires, not like wheels. In you, what corresponds to moving wheels are your moving muscles.

You can do many things a car cannot. You can, for example, lift your arm to comb your hair; you can talk; you can hear; you can use the camera which is your eyes. Really you have a double camera, for not only can you see what is before you, but also you can imagine what is going on elsewhere, seeing

this also. In other words, you can have visual images of what
is or may be going on elsewhere. While talking with one person, you often see in imagination what some other person might
say or do. This is mental activity.

The automobile does not engage in mental activity. Its
wheels do not enable it to think. Your muscles enable you to
think. This you will discover for yourself later on.

As you learn to control the operations of your muscles,
including the minute ones which always are employed when
you think, you are learning self-operations control. Mind and
body are one operating unit, not two. This operating unit
always is based on muscle contraction.

Where are your controls? They must be where you can get
at them to operate. You will find that they are in your muscles!
To make this discovery, bend back your left hand. While doing
this, notice the delicate sensation signal you get in the muscles
in the upper surface of your left forearm. This signal will be
largely absent in the right forearm, if you keep this arm at
ease. Compare the two regions, so as to note the signal present
in the left forearm when you are bending the left hand back,
but absent on the right, when not bending.

Once more, note carefully the sensation-signal thus present
on the left. This is the control we have been looking for. There
are many ways to use this signal profitably for your efficiency.

Over-all View

A car has four wheels which move together and which you
control when you drive. You have over 1,000 muscles which
never move together when under control but which move in
the most complex patterns and networks in accordance with
your purposes.

In each of your muscles the controls which you can learn to
operate lie inside the tiny fibers. These are in spindles so small
that they can be seen only if magnified under a microscope
(See Figure 1). There are thousands of controls in each
muscle, yet you can learn to operate the muscles if you learn

to recognize the control sensation-signals. These are present when the muscle fibers shorten. They are absent when the fibers lengthen. Their absence is what we shall call relaxation. There is no positive signal of being relaxed.

You will not need to learn how to operate each and every muscle individually, but in groups.

Chart for Learning

You are to learn how to get power on and off in groups of muscles according to what you are doing. For sleep, you want power off in all muscles directly under your control. Indeed, this is sleep in its most restful form. At any moment of daily activities, you want power on in those muscle groups needed for what you are doing but power off in those not needed. Thus you avoid waste of vital energies, avert fatigue, wear and tear and save yourself generally. We call this *differential control*.

Chart for Thorough Course

In the lying position, the order of learning (a) to distinguish the control signal in each chief muscle group and thereupon (b) to go off with the power is as follows: Left Arm: 7 days; right arm: 7 days; left leg, 10 days; right leg, 10 days; trunk, 10 days; neck; 6 days; eye-region, 12 days; visualization, 9 days; speech region, 19 days.

In the sitting position, the same order and the same duration are required.

You are to proceed from one muscle group to the following, in order of the drawings on pages 14 to 32 inclusive. Generally, you practice one tension per hour-period. You are to perform this one tension three times. As a rule this is all you do in a single hour. You do not practice several different tensions in a single hour.

Briefer Course

In a shortened course, you spend less time on each part. One way of abridgement is to perform Arm 1, Arm 2 and Arm 3 in 1 hour, instead of 3 hours. Under this regimen, for example, in one hour-period you will bend your hand back 3 times with 5-minute rests in between, then forward 3 times with 5-minute rests in between and finally go negative, relaxing the whole forearm for the last 25 minutes of the hour. Guess at the time intervals. Do not follow your watch.

Similar abridgement can be performed in practice on the legs and other parts of the body. Thus, the course can be shortened to 1/3 of the time employed for a more thorough course. However, in this as in other important tasks of life, thoroughness pays off.

Once you have learned to observe your effort tensions and to get power off where not needed in any task, you do not have to keep your mind on it, for it becomes second nature to run your organism efficiently, just as you learn to drive a car.

Read directions for Arm Practice on page 14. If you practice an hour a day, in the unabridged course your first day will be devoted exclusively to Left Arm 1. Then 14 days will be required to cover both arms.

General Plan for Learning

The general plan for learning will be illustrated in the following directions for your first period. Read the directions and look at the drawing for Left Arm 1 on page 14. You will find 8 instructions for steps to be followed *consecutively* during the hour-period. You are to take 8 similar steps in Period No. 2, except that in Period 2 you are to bend the left hand forward instead of backwards.

The same eight instructions will apply during every period of the entire course, except that the act performed will vary with the number of the period, as shown by the drawings.

This rule will not hold for every third time you practice, for in this hour you should omit tensing altogether. Simply relax only. In this way you will avoid forming the wrong habit of tensing a part before you begin to relax it. For examples, note that in Left Arm Period 3 and Period 6 you are not to tense at all.

Your First Period

To make a beginning, read the instructions for Left Arm 1 on page 14. Also, read what is said below on pages 7 to 11 which applies to all periods of practice. Then lie down on a couch or bed alone in a room with doors closed. Avoid being called during the hour.*

Let your arms rest at your sides, your hands a little away from your body, and do not cross your legs. Leave your eyes open for 3 or 4 minutes and then close them gradually. Guess at the time; do not look at any clock or watch.

Bend Left Hand Back. Why?

When your eyes have remained closed for an estimated 3 or 4 minutes more, bend back your left hand at the wrist steadily, without fluctuation. Do not seesaw. While doing so, with care you can note a vague misty sensation in the upper surface of your left forearm. You may call it "tightness." This is the signal of tension, the control, which you are to learn to recognize, just as a telegrapher must learn to recognize sound-signals.

Avoid Prolonged Attention to Tension Signals

Do not give prolonged attention to the control signal. Some people mistakenly keep watching their tension signals during the entire hour of practice. Thereby they do not really go negative, for really they are keeping their eyes continually busy in the act of attention to muscle signals and this triggers tension over their entire musculature.

Control Signal vs. Strain Signal

Distinguish the signal of tension from the stronger signal of *strain* at the wrist. The strain signal in the wrist stands out more. However, you can not run yourself by strains, any more

---

* Do not interrupt the practice to read. However, after your first hour of practice, read the instructions mentioned once again, for then they will mean more to you.

than a motor car can be driven by strains on the motor. What is important for running yourself is the control signal in and from the muscle. It informs you, however grossly, when and where you are expending effort-energy. Besides, the controls are important if you want to learn self-engineering—just as important as are the control devices on the dashboard of your car if you want to drive it.

Repetition Required

Once more, then, bend your left hand back in order to observe the control sensation again. This is going on with the power exactly where you note the muscle signal, which is where you are performing work.

No Switch and No Effort to Relax

To go off requires no turning of a switch, for there is no switch. It is far simpler than when you switch off the electric light. Then work is required to move the switch (work is forces times distance).

However, no work is required to go off with the power in your forearm. All you need to do is to *discontinue* working there. No effort is required. An effort to relax is failure to relax. Untrained people often fail to relax because they work to relax.

To tense requires continuous effort-work so long as tensing is maintained. The moment you discontinue tensing (without effort to do so) you relax. This is *power off*, going negative. All you need to do is to discontinue working. It is simple and easy.

Many people ask, "What shall I think about when I lie down?" Please read the following answer more than once: You are not told to think and you are not told to make your mind a blank! During Practice Period 1 and during following practice periods, if you find yourself thinking about yourself, your practice or anything else, go off with the power in the muscle regions on which you are now practicing or have practiced in foregoing periods. If the thinking recurs, go negative again, no matter how often.

Avoid Autosuggestion and Hypnosis

Do not tell yourself in words, "This will make me feel fine!" If, at the close of any practice period you are pleased and tell yourself, "I felt as if floating!", the truth is that you have not really relaxed but instead have engaged in autosuggestive fantasy. Such procedures render you dependent on words or on hypnotists. In self-engineering, autosuggestion and hypnosis have no place whatsoever. Therefore, read the directions again and follow them carefully.

Control Progresses

In practicing going negative in any muscle, go negative likewise in the parts on which you have practiced in preceding periods.

Residual Tension

As you will find, tension, like a conflagration, does not go to zero readily. When anybody lies down, including your cat or dog, measurements show that tension does not subside to zero as a rule. On the contrary, some tension tends to persist unnecessarily in every muscle. This is called *residual tension.* Because residual tension tends to be with you always, you need have no concern that our practices will make you too relaxed. No one ever learns to draw a perfect circle or to play golf perfectly and no one ever learns to relax perfectly. Whatever the skill you develop in tension control, there will always remain a great gap between the point you reach and perfection. Have no fear that tension control ever will make you lazy!

In Practice Period 7, after relaxing the entire left arm for about 5 minutes with eyes closed, begin to stiffen the entire left arm without moving even a finger. Proceed to stiffen very gradually, continuously (without sudden increments) increasing the rigidity. This will not be what we want until you have learned to take several minutes to perform the increase uniformly.

Do not stiffen your arm to the point of extreme effort but only in moderation. When the arm has very gradually become moderately tense or rigid, begin to go negative very, very slowly and gradually. The instruction is: Whatever you have done up to this point in stiffening your arm, begin now to do it a very little less and gradually less, less and less, even up to and beyond the point where the arm appears to you to be quite relaxed, i.e., perfectly free from control signal. You can safely assume that even at this point you are still engaging at least a little in residual tensing. Accordingly, whatever you have been doing negatively up to this point, continue on negatively further and further for another 10 or 15 minutes. But make no effort to hold still or to relax.

Analogous progressive relaxation instructions apply to Period 14, Right Arm, Period 10, Left Leg, and so on.

Tension Control During Hours of Daily Activity

To some extent, your gains in tension control from practice lying down will be transferred into your daily habits at work and at play. This will occur automatically. As you learn, it becomes second nature. However, while fully relaxed muscles are not needed during any occupation (indeed would render such activity impossible), some degree of control can improve your efficiency during any type of occupation. Watch yourself occasionally, however briefly, to see if you are excessively vigorous even in the tensions needed to carry out your purposes. Do you grasp your pen or pencil very tightly when you write? Do you talk too loudly or too long from overtension? Are your eyes always looking? These tensions are called *primary* because they are needed. However, if they are overvigorous, you are paying too big a price in energy reserves. You should relax these tensions but only partially, because you need them for your job or pleasure. Do you doodle? If so, this is tension called *secondary* because it is not needed. Any secondary tension has nuisance value only and should be relaxed completely.

Need To Observe Faintest Control Signal

You are to learn to recognize very faint control signals. Why? It is important because you have built-in equipment for performing major efforts based on faint controls. To sign a binding contract requires little effort energy, notwithstanding that the consequences may affect your entire subsequent fortunes and existence. Your tensions in signing a contract or engaging in any other significant effort-pattern evidently do not depend on their intensity for the importance of their consequences. Like the signals of the telegrapher's keys, it is the pattern rather than the strength of signals which conveys the significance.

In a word, self-operations control is the science for living which depends on recognizing and employing the faintest effort-signals in the interest of practical welfare.

If You Fall Asleep

You are not requested to try to go to sleep during your practice periods or to try to stay awake, but, if you should fall asleep as you go negative, there is no objection.

VISUALIZATION AND SPEECH

Follow the directions on visualization on page 26 and on subsequent days those on speech on pages 27 to 29 inclusive. To learn the significance of these practices and how they can help you to save your mental energies, read the section on pages 11 to 12 entitled Control of Mind. It is well to read this section more than once, not only before you begin the visualization practice, but also again afterwards. Also, you might profitably read this section repeatedly before and after the days devoted to attaining skill in observing and controlling tensions of the speech muscles.

CONTROL OF MIND

When you think or imagine or engage in any other form of mental activity, your brain is active, but to no greater extent than when you engage in any so-called physical activity, such as golf. Without a brain you could not think, but neither could you play golf. At no time do you feel your brain working; neither do you ever have tension signals in the brain. As you learn to recognize tensions, you will find them chiefly in the eyes and speech regions on thinking, but not in the brain.

You can learn to control your thinking and emotions to a useful extent because these mental activities occur only if and when you tense your eye and speech muscles. However, you may use also every other muscle in your body in thinking and in emotion, depending on the patterns which correspond to your endeavors.

Electrical measurements show, for instance, that people use their arm muscles often in imagination.

Close your eyes and think about any matter. If skilled, you will notice (1) visual pictures, called images, but also (2) eye tensions to look at what you see in imagination. In thinking, also, you are likely to use your speech apparatus to form words, but these are not spoken aloud. Electrical measurements disclose that you use the same muscles as you use in saying the same words aloud.

However, you should discover for yourself (on following the instructions for visualization and for speech on pp. 26 to 29 inclusive), that the tension signals and the image signals are delicate, fleeting and greatly abbreviated. Otherwise, in visual imagination you look at the objects you think about, turning your eyes in the same way as if you were looking at real objects.

Thus, imagination is a shorthand, a telescopic reproduction in which you use your muscles just as you do in reality when you see objects or persons and speak aloud. However, in mental activity the tensions are miniscule. As said above, you will find that all other muscles may and do participate in some of your tension-image patterns.

When you engage in any mental or physical effort, the brain and the muscles act approximately simultaneously. That the brain has an idea first which later is expressed in the muscles is an incorrect view for which no evidence ever was presented, although many people held it and still do.

When Muscle Power Is Off

At any moment if the muscles either of the arms or legs or trunk are really relaxed approximately to zero tension, the mind is thereby quieted. Why? Because in thinking or emotion, tensions in the parts mentioned participate. They are the actors in any and every play of the mind. Without them participating, the mind is vacant.

Understanding this will enable you to apprehend why "the mind relaxes" when the limbs or trunk or any other larger section of the body relaxes. However, remember that for this the tension-signals must be reduced to zero or nearly so. If the reduction falls short, leaving tension signals of a diminished but sufficient order, then, as when the telegrapher's signals are still faintly present, the messages are still there and the mind keeps on working. See Figure 2, below.

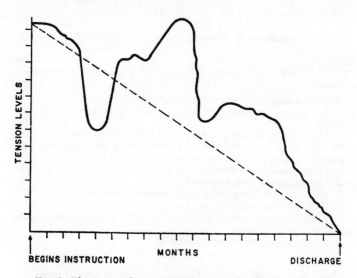

Fɪɢ. 2. This is one of many possible curves that illustrate that you should not expect uninterrupted improvement. The course of improvement never runs smooth but, generally, is marked by ups and downs. There will be times of discouragement and relapse but these offer valuable opportunities to learn how to meet difficult moments.

ARM PRACTICE

In each hour-practice period, follow the appropriate photograph, performing the tension indicated 3 times at intervals of several minutes. These are NOT exercises. Interest yourself in becoming familiar with the control sensation in each part so that you can learn really to run yourself properly relaxed under all conditions.

PERIODS	LEFT ARM	PERIODS	RIGHT ARM
1.	Bend hand back.	8.	Bend hand back.
2.	Bend hand forward.	9.	Bend hand forward.
3.	Relax only.	10.	Relax only.
4.	Bend at elbow.	11.	Bend at elbow.
5.	Press wrist down on books.	12.	Press wrist down on books.
6.	Relax only.	13.	Relax only.
7.	Progressive tension and relaxation of whole	14.	Progressive tension and relaxation of whole arm

Arm 1   **Lying**

PERIOD No. 1

Select a quiet room, free from intruders and phone calls.

1. Lying on your back with arms at sides, leave eyes open 3 to 4 minutes.

2. Gradually close eyes and keep them closed entire hour.

3. After 3 to 4 minutes with eyes closed, bend left hand back (see photograph), observing the control sensation 1 to 2 minutes and how it differs from the strains in the wrist and in the lower portion of the forearm.

4. Go negative for 3 to 4 minutes.

5. Again bend left hand back and observe as previously.

6. Once more go negative 3 to 4 minutes.

7. Bend left hand back a third and last time, observing the control sensation 1 to 2 minutes.

8. Finally go negative for remainder of hour.

Arm 1: Lying
Bend hand back. (Felt in back upper part of forearm)

Arm 2: Lying
Bend hand forward. (Felt in front of forearm)

Arm 3   **Lying**

Period No. 3

Lie quietly on back as previously, arms at sides. In this *and in all subsequent periods lying down,* leave eyes open several minutes, then gradually close them and *keep closed* for entire hour. Throughout this period go negative only: Do not bend, extend or stiffen the arm; but if you should do so, awaredly or unawaredly, note the slight control sensation which will thereupon appear in the left arm and go negative there at once.

Do not tense to relax.

In General

Period No. 3 is called a zero period.

Hereafter, every third period is to be a zero period. In other practice periods, specialize on one tension only, performing the three times.

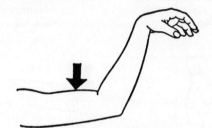

Arm 4: Lying
Bend arm at elbow, about 35°. (Felt in biceps, front of upper arm)

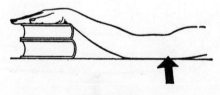

Arm 5: Lying
Press wrist down against books. (Felt in back part of upper arm)

LEG PRACTICE   Lying

In each daily practice period, follow the appropriate photograph, performing the tension indicated 3 times at intervals of several minutes. These are *NOT* exercises. Interest yourself in becoming familiar with the control sensation in each part so that you can learn really to run yourself properly relaxed under all conditions.

DAY	LEFT LEG	DAY	RIGHT LEG
1.	Bend foot up.	11.	Bend foot up.
2.	Bend foot down.	12.	Bend foot down.
3.	Relax only.	13.	Relax only.
4.	Raise foot.	14.	Raise foot.
5.	Bend at knee.	15.	Bend at knee.
6.	Relax only.	16.	Relax only.
7.	Raise knee.	17.	Raise knee.
8.	Press lower thigh down.	18.	Press lower thigh down.
9.	Relax entire left leg.	19.	Relax entire right knee.
10.	Progressive tension and relaxation of entire left leg.	20.	Progressive tension and relaxation of entire right leg.

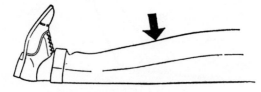

Leg 1: Lying
Bend foot up. (Felt along front of lower leg)

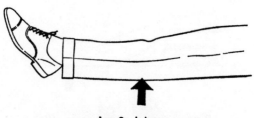

Leg 2: Lying
Extend foot. (Felt in calf)

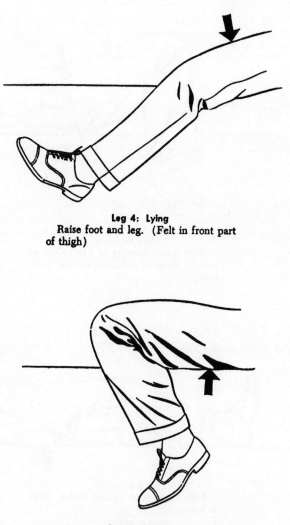

Leg 4: Lying
Raise foot and leg. (Felt in front part
of thigh)

Leg 5: Lying
Bend leg at knee. (Felt along back of
thigh)

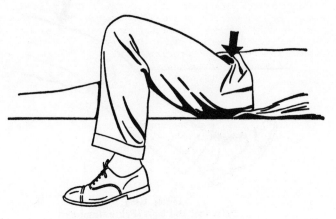

Leg 7: Lying
Raise knee, bending at hip. (Felt in muscles deep in abdomen, toward back, near hip)

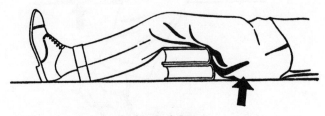

Leg 8: Lying
Press lower thigh against books. (Felt in buttocks)

TRUNK PRACTICE

In each daily practice period, follow the appropriate photograph, performing the tension indicated 3 times at intervals of several minutes. These are *NOT* exercises. Interest yourself in becoming familiar with the control sensation in each part so that you can learn really to run yourself properly relaxed under all conditions.

DAY TRUNK
1. Pull in abdomen.
2. Arch back slightly.
3. Relax abdomen, back and legs.
4. Observe during a deeper breath.
5. Bend shoulders back.
6. Relax only.
7. Left arm forward and inward.
8. Right arm forward and inward.
9. Relax only.
10. Elevate shoulders.

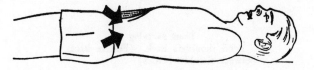

Trunk 1: Lying
Pull in abdomen. (Felt faintly all over abdomen)

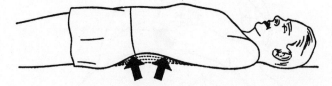

Trunk 2: Lying
Arch the back. (Felt definitely along both sides of the spine)

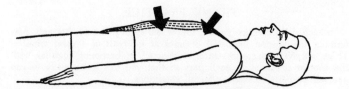

Trunk 4: Lying
Observe during a deeper breath. (Very
faint diffuse tenseness felt all over chest)

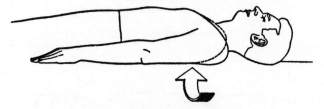

Trunk 5: Lying
Bend shoulders back. (Felt in back,
between shoulder blades)

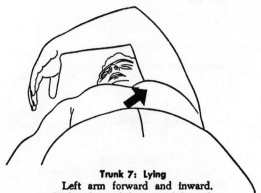

Trunk 7: Lying
Left arm forward and inward.
(Felt in front of chest near left arm)

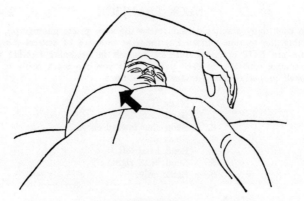

Trunk 8: Lying
Right arm forward and inward. (Felt
in front of chest on right)

Trunk 10: Lying
Elevate shoulders. (Felt along top of
shoulders and in sides of neck)

NECK PRACTICE   Lying

In each daily practice period, follow the appropriate photograph, performing the tension indicated 3 times at intervals of several minutes. These are *NOT* exercises. Interest yourself in becoming familiar with the control sensation in each part so that you can learn really to run yourself properly relaxed under all conditions.

Day	Neck, Lying
1.	Bend head back.
2.	Bend chin toward chest.
3.	Relax only.
4.	Bend head left.
5.	Bend head right.
6.	Relax only.

Neck 1: Lying
Bend head back. (Felt in back of neck, perhaps below, in back)

Neck 2: Lying
Bend chin down. (Felt in sides of neck)

Neck 3: Lying
Relax only.

Neck 4: Lying
Bend head left. (Felt in left side of neck)

Neck 5: Lying
Bend head right. (Felt
in right side of neck)

Neck 6: Lying
Relax only.

EYE REGION PRACTICE

In each daily practice period, follow the appropriate photograph, performing the tension indicated 3 times at intervals of several minutes. These are *NOT* exercises. Interest yourself in becoming familiar with the control sensation in each part so that you can learn really to run yourself properly relaxed under all conditions.

DAY   EYE REGION
1. Wrinkle forehead.
2. Frown.
3. Relax only.
4. Close eyelids tightly.
5. Look left with lids closed.
6. Relax only.
7. Look right with lids closed.
8. Look up.
9. Relax only.
10. Look downward with lids closed.
11. Look forward with lids closed.
12. Relax only.

Eye Region 1: Lying
Wrinkle forehead.
(Felt diffusely over
entire forehead)

Eye Region 2: Lying
Frown. (Felt distinctly between eyes)

Eye Region 4: Lying
Close eyelids
tightly. (Felt all
over eyelids)

Eye Region 5: Lying
Look up (eyelids
closed). (Felt in eyeball muscles at top;
tensions change rapidly as eyes move)

Eye Region 7: Lying
Look right (eyelids closed). (Felt in eyeball muscles, right; note static and moving tensions)

Eye Region 8: Lying
Look left (eyelids closed). (Felt in eyeball muscles, left)

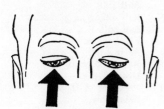

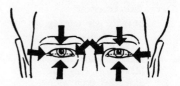

Eye Region 10: Lying
Look down (eyelids closed). (Felt in eyeball muscles, below)

Eye Region 11: Lying
Look forward (eyelids closed). (Felt in muscles all around eyeballs)

VISUALIZATION PRACTICE
With lids open
With lids closed

In each daily practice period, follow the appropriate photograph, performing the tension indicated 3 times at intervals of several minutes. These are *NOT* exercises. Interest yourself in becoming familiar with the control sensation in each part so that you can learn really to run yourself properly relaxed under all conditions.

DAY	VISUALIZATION
1.	Imagine pen moving side to side.
	Make it go very slowly.
	Make it stand still.
	Make it go very fast.
2.	Skyrocket train passing quickly.
	Man walking by.
3.	Relax eyes to zero.

DAY	VISUALIZATION
4.	Bird flying from tree to tree.
	Bird still.
5.	Ball rolling on ground.
	Ball still.
	Eiffel tower.
6.	Relax only.
7.	Rabbit on road.
	Head of pin.
8.	President of U. S.
9.	Relax only.

SPEECH REGION PRACTICE

In each daily practice period, follow the appropriate photograph, performing the tension indicated 3 times at intervals of several minutes. These are *NOT* exercises. Interest yourself in becoming familiar with the control sensation in each part so that you can learn really to run yourself properly relaxed under all conditions.

DAY
1. Close jaws somewhat firmly.
2. Open jaws.
3. Relax only.
4. Show teeth (as if smiling).
5. Pout.
6. Relax only.
7. Push tongue forward against teeth.
8. Pull tongue backward.
9. Relax only.
10. Count to 10.
11. Count half as loudly.
12. Relax only.

DAY
13. Count very faintly.
14. Count imperceptibly.
15. Relax only.
16. Imagine that you are counting.
17. Imagine you are saying alphabet.
18. Relax only.
19. Imagine saying name three times.
    Address three times.
    Name of President three times.

Speech Region 1: Lying
Close jaws rather firmly. (Felt at back of lower jaw and in temples)

Speech Region 2: Lying
Open jaws. (Felt in sides of lower jaw and neck)

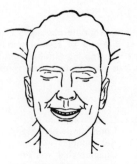

Speech Region 4: Lying
Show teeth (as if
smiling). (Felt in
cheeks)

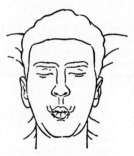

Speech Region 5: Lying
Pout. (Felt in and
around lips)

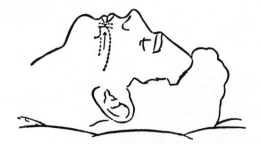

Speech Region 7: Lying
Push tongue against teeth. (Felt in
tongue)

Speech Region 8: Lying
Pull tongue back-
wards. (Felt in
tongue and floor of
mouth)

Speech Region 10: Lying
Count to 10. (Felt
in cheeks, lips,
tongue, jaw muscles,
throat, chest and,
perhaps, abdomen)

Arm 1: Sitting
Bend hand back. (Felt in
back part of forearm)

Arm 2: Sitting
Bend hand down. (Felt in
front part of forearm)

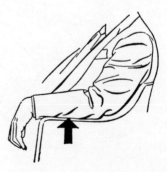

Arm 4: Sitting
Bend arm at elbow. (Felt
in biceps, front of upper arm)

Arm 5: Sitting
Press wrist down against
arm of chair. (Felt in back,
upper arm)

Leg 1: Sitting
Bend foot up. (Felt along
front of lower leg)

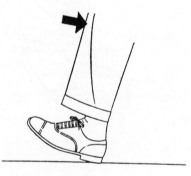

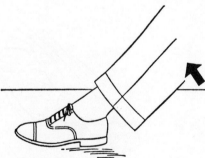

Leg 2: Sitting
Press toe end of foot
down. (Felt in calf)

Leg 4: Sitting
Raise foot without moving
thigh. (Felt in front of thigh)

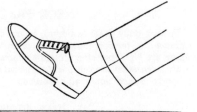

Leg 5: Sitting
Pull heel back
without moving
thigh. (Felt along
back of thigh)

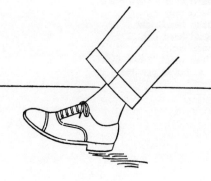

Leg 7: Sitting
Press down whole
foot. (Felt in buttocks)

Leg 8: Sitting
Raise knee while foot
hangs limply. (Felt in
psoas muscles deep in ab-
domen, toward back)

NECK PRACTICE   Sitting

In each daily practice period, follow the appropriate photograph, performing the tension indicated 3 times at intervals of several minutes. These are *NOT* exercises. Interest yourself in becoming familiar with the control sensation in each part so that you can learn really to run yourself properly relaxed under all conditions.

DAY   NECK, SITTING
1.   Bend head back slightly.
2.   Bend chin toward chest.
3.   Relax only.
4.   Bend head right.
5.   Bend head left.
6.   Relax only.
7.   Head erect. Relax neck
      as far as possible.

JOSEPH O'CONNOR

Guitar Playing

As I sit down to write this, with a blank piece of paper in front of me, I feel rather like a composer might feel when given a theme to work on. 'Tensions in the performance of music' is a multifaceted theme. The more viewpoints and feelings about it, the richer the result. I plan to improvise a variation on the theme for guitar.

Thinking about tension, what comes to my mind first is an image of a tightrope walker. I love the circus and have vivid memories of circus performers and circus visits when I was young. I remember the tightrope walker high above us, brightly dressed, balanced on the thin, stretched wire holding the long balancing pole in front of him. Although he would sway one way and then the other, every step was precise. We, the audience were tense, it was as if we were walking with him, sharing in his adventure. He might even have played on our feelings, by pretending to lose balance, before regaining it by swaying the other way. Then the whole audience would gasp in unison. When he reached the other end, we would applaud in appreciation and relief, now we could relax.

There is a saying that there are three types of performance. The one you prepared, the one you gave and the one you wished you had given. 'Tension' often gets the blame for the gap between the second and the third. We sometimes make a distinction between two types of tension, tension in the body, inhibiting a free, effective technique on the instrument, and emotional tension, meaning a poor emotional state and inability to concentrate. Put them together and you get what is known as performance anxiety or 'stage fright'. However this is an artificial distinction. The body and mind are parts of one system, so the two types of tension always go hand in hand, regardless of the one you are most aware of.

I invite you to think about tension in a slightly different way here. The word 'tension' is what linguists call a nominalisation. It is an abstract noun, and does not exist as a thing in reality, it is a useful shorthand way of describing what someone is doing, or creating. It makes no sense to say, 'I have too much tension'. To do so makes it more difficult to deal with, because you are turning a process into a thing and placing it apart from you, as if it is something that is happening to you instead of something you are actively creating. Tension is a useful word, I use it to describe the difference you create between two states. Think of a guitar string. It is useless when completely slack, stretch it too far and the note will be out of tune, eventually the string will snap. Too much tension and the note is sharp, too slack, the note is flat. The right amount of tension produces the right note. The right difference between the 'relaxed' state of the string, and the stretch you subject it to. Without tension or difference, there can be no resolution and no music.

Physical Tension
Taking physical tension first. To carry out any physical movement whether it be large movements, such as walking, or much finer movements such as striking a guitar string, some muscles need to contract. There will be an optimum balance where certain muscles are contracted and certain muscles are relaxed. Muscles that contract when they do not need to, or contract to a greater degree than needed will create 'tension'. Tension is the difference between the amount of muscle contraction you need, and the amount you actually use.

When I think of guitar technique, I think in terms of dynamic balance, and playing with the least amount of physical effort. I ask myself 'What looks unbalanced in the body and hands that needs to be balanced?' Not enough tension in this sense is as bad as too much. So the question becomes 'How much tension do you want and where do you want it?'

The classical guitarist's posture is a good example of dynamic physical balance and muscle co-ordination. Although the fingers strike the strings, the guitar is played with the whole body, fingers do not exist in isolation. The fingers are brought into contact with the strings by the hand, positioned by the arms, which rest on the guitar depending on the position of the torso and back. The whole body weight will either be balanced evenly or be leaning one way. So technical problems show themselves in the fingers, but always need to be corrected by balancing larger muscle groups: arms, shoulders, or back.

Posture, that is how the whole body is held, will effect how the guitar is held and how the fingers move. I treat the hold on the instrument as part of the overall posture. So posture is critical, and yet comparatively little time is spent on it. This is understandable, both teacher and student are eager to play music right from the beginning. The first lesson is when the student's enthusiasm is at its greatest, so that is exactly the time to make sure fundamental issues like posture are considered. Once posture is dealt with, both teacher and student have an experience to refer back to. Posture has to be imprinted on muscle memory. Demonstrations are also useful, the student can model the teacher. Students need to be guided and shown, rather than talked into guitar posture. Words are inadequate to convey bodily feelings and balance, so I will not attempt to describe guitar posture or the hold on the instrument fully, only give some guidelines.

Most classical guitarists raise the left leg six inches or so by resting it on a small footstool. The guitar then rests with its lower bout on the left thigh (see illustration). It is kept stable by its contact with the right inside leg, the top of the left thigh, and the chest. The right arm rests on the upper edge of the guitar body, and the weight of the arm keeps the guitar in place. If the right arm were removed, the guitar would tip over to the left. (I am describing playing the guitar in the standard right handed way). Good guitar posture means the body is balanced, upright, and comfortable, and the guitar is held stable. As an alternative to the footstool, the 'guitar cushion' is becoming increasingly popular. This is a firm, shaped cushion placed on top of the left leg, and the guitar is rested on that. This dispenses with the footstool. It raises and angles the guitar and allows the guitarist to keep both feet on the floor, avoiding extra stress on the back from raising one leg with the footstool, and not the other. I favour the cushion for this reason, but it will not be right for everybody. Sometimes a combination of a low footstool together with a cushion works best of all, especially for tall guitarists.

One way of checking if your body is balanced, upright and comfortable is to imagine what you would look like if suddenly, by magic, the guitar disappeared. How long could you maintain your position then? Would it look strange to someone who had just walked into the room?

Guitarists tend to be prone to backache, usually due to twisting the head and upper back to the left, to look at the left hand. It is not necessary to focus fully on the left hand. Peripheral vision, (the vision from the corners of the eye) is quite adequate in most cases, and, if you are sufficiently upright, with the guitar at a steep enough angle, you can see the left hand without twisting the body; you need only turn the head. You do not need to stare at the fingerboard full face to see it clearly. Another cause of backache is to slump over the guitar, the lower back is rounded outwards, putting pressure on the base of the spine.

It is also important to use a chair of the right height. The chair must be high enough to allow you to place both feet

flat on the floor, making a right angle between your upper and lower leg. The chair's height will be roughly the distance from the bottom of your heel to the top of your knee.

The right arm, will normally rest on the top edge of the guitar somewhere between elbow and wrist. The exact point on the arm depends on a number of factors: the length of the guitarist's arms, how short his fingers, and how large the guitar. It is important however, that the guitarist supports the forearm and not the upper arm. Without this support the guitarist will have to hold up their forearm, it will be unbalanced like a long lever that has a fulcrum at one end instead of towards the middle.

An effective sitting position will be comfortable and easy to maintain for a reasonable practise time. Bad posture will cause technical difficulties with the instrument, and usually some pain after a while, usually in the lower back. However even with good posture, I believe it is important to take frequent breaks, and not practice for longer than about three quarters of an hour at a time. Then take a fifteen minute break, move the body and do something different for a while, before returning to play. Practice sessions pay dimininshing returns after about three quarters of an hour. And after an hour, mental fatigue if not physical fatigue sets in and renders practice very inefficient. Far better to do two sessions of an hour with a break, than two hours with no break. More is not necessarily better. A break helps the mind and body to rest, and consolidates the memories of what has been learnt.[1]

An effective playing position will be comfortable, but not vice versa: a comfortable position is not necessarily effective. This is sometimes forgotten by students. For example I am comfortable leaning back in a chair, but to try and play the guitar like that would be very ineffective, and would probably create strains in my hands and fingers.

The guitar must be held steady. Unless it is held firmly, it

[1]   *The Brain Book* Peter Russell (*Routledge & Kegan Paul 1979*)

will shift and slip making good playing impossible. So if the guitarist's basic posture allows the guitar to be unstable, the player will tend to do one (or both) of two other actions in an attempt to stabilise it. The first is to push the guitar inwards with the right arm or right wrist. This sets up a counterpressure pushing the right shoulder forwards and out. The arm will be stiff and the right wrist collapsed. The result is usually a poor, weak sound and eventual pain in the shoulder and neck.

The second attempted solution to keep the guitar steady, is to grip the neck with the left hand. Then the left hand will not be able to stretch either across, or up the fingerboard because the more the thumb comes round the neck, the more the fingers are drawn together. Secondly shifting the left hand up or down the neck will be difficult, because it dare not relax its grip for fear that the guitar will move.

Bending the thumb round the guitar neck puts the player's hand into the 'power grip', opposing the fingers as a group against the thumb, rather than the 'precision grip' which opposes the fingers independently. Very often changing the posture will stop students using the power grip, they no longer need to, the guitar is steady already. To attempt to change from power to precision grip without paying attention to the rest of the body will seldom work. A 'power grip' results in a clumsy left hand technique. Musicianship, interpretation, the 'presence' of the player are essential. Music is about the beauty of sound, and sometimes dealing with small points of posture seems far removed from music. Yes, music is to do with beauty of sound, and without an adequate technique the beauty of the sound will suffer. Technique is the means to the end of creating beautiful music. It is absolutely necessary, though not sufficient for a good performance. It must be there to communicate your ideas and interpretation to the audience.

What can a teacher do to help a student maintain a good posture? There are many different ways. I want to focus on one point I have found useful. It is important to give positive instructions. Tell the student what to do, not what not to do. Two reasons. A series of comments about what someone is doing wrong can be endless and does not do much to enhance rapport. We learn by a series of 'successive approximations' so are unlikely to get anything absolutely right the first time, there is always room for improvement. Moving a student towards what works, avoids what can be perceived as endless fault finding. Good posture needs constant reinforcement. It does take time to establish good posture so that it is habitual. Sometimes students have poor postural habits. You can change a student's posture, but it will often revert just as quickly. (As Mark Twain said, 'Giving up smoking is easy, I do it every day.') Habits take time to build and take time to change. If I find myself needing to remind students about posture I often reframe my concern about correct posture by saying something like, 'Posture is really important and I want to reassure you that you can always rely on me to remind you if you need to adjust it.') This reframe can avoid being perceived as nagging, until good postural habits are installed. On the other hand, some students will adopt an excellent posture right from the beginning.

There is a story[2] that anthropologist Gregory Bateson tells about a conversation he had with his young daughter. Her question was, 'Why do things always get in a muddle? Why is it so hard to keep things tidy?' He responded by asking her what would happen if he moved various objects in the room to different places. She said it would make the room untidy. Eventually he said, 'It's not that it's more difficult to keep things tidy, it's just that there are far more ways for things to be untidy than there are for them to be tidy.' There are many, many ways the guitar can be held that are not very effective and very few that are balanced, effective, and relaxed.

---

[2] *Steps Towards an Ecology of Mind* Gregory Bateson (*Ballantine Books 1972*)

The worst thing you can do is to give a student a stream of instructions on what not to do. Just as the famous order, 'Don't think of the colour blue?' makes it impossible to obey the instruction without disobeying it, so directing the student's attention to the things they must not do, focuses their attention on just those things and makes them more likely to happen.

Emotional State

Tension is often used as a shorthand for the cause (or result?) of a poor emotional state. Again I would like to invite you to think of the word 'tension' a little differently in this context too. We speak of being 'tensed up' in readiness for a performance. Yet most performers report they need to feel an edge of excitement to give a good performance. In this sense, tension is not a bad thing that should be simply eliminated. The analogy of a guitar string comes to my mind again. Slackening the string does not make the sound better. There is only a problem if the performer gets into a state where they are too anxious or upset to perform well. As mind and body are one system, emotional tension will always be associated with some physiological change: common ones are excessive muscle contraction, sweating, increased pulse, or trembling. This is stage fright or performance anxiety and can occur regardless of the preparation done, the hours spent practising.

So some feeling of excitement, anticipation, and mental and physical readiness is helpful. Anything more than this, interfering with your performance I would call 'tension' when applied to emotional state.

I prepare many students for performing, either for examinations or concerts. Emotional state is the single greatest influence on quality of the performance, given they have prepared the music adequately. In examinations, the emotional state of the candidate can easily account for 20% of the marks either way, and make the difference between pass or fail. It is an important part of my task to give students some ways of accessing and maintaining a good state for their performance. Otherwise performance situations can easily get anchored to a feeling of fear. Creative imagery is used a great deal by teachers and therapists with good results to deal with emotional states. I would like to sketch out a process here that uses imagery together with Neuro-Linguistics[3], that can be used to feel more resourceful in a performance situation. I will describe it from a teacher's point of view, but it can easily be modified for use without a teacher.

The first stage if you are working with a student is to make sure you have rapport. Tell them what you intend to do and how important it is. Make it fun and interesting.

Find out if the student is worried about being nervous in the examination. If so, ask them *how they would rather feel*. Get a positive state (eg. confidence, relaxation, pleasantly excited), and not just an absence of nerves. Any approach that tries to remove performance nerves without giving some positive alternative falls into the 'Don't think of the colour blue!' trap.

The next stage is to get them to think of a past time when they did not feel in this positive state. It need have nothing to do with the guitar, music, or examinations. You need know nothing about the situation they think of. All that matters is that it was a time when they felt how they want to feel in the performance. If they have difficulty, get them to think how a role model might feel, or to just imagine how they would like to feel. It makes no difference as long as they have a way into that feeling.

Then ask them to see an image in their mind that will remind them strongly of this positive feeling. Next, ask them to hear something, (eg. a word or a sound, or music), that links with the feeling. Lastly, to think of some gesture

[3]   Accessing and anchoring resourceful states is dealt with more fully in: *Introducing Neuro-Linguistic Programming* Joseph O'Connor and John Seymour (HarperCollins 1990)

that is small and unobtrusive (eg. clenching a fist), they can associate with the feeling.

Ask them to go back strongly into the positive state and re-experience the resourceful feeling. Notice what they look like when they are feeling like this, (for example skin colour, breathing pattern, balance, where they are looking), so you can recognise it again. This is called calibration. It is the way you will be able to tell if the student really does feel resourceful later, because you have a mental image of how they look when feeling resourceful. When the resourceful feeling is at its height, they are to see the image, hear the sound or word, and make the gesture. Give them all the time they need to do this.

Next you will need to distract their attention so you can test the association. When they have come out of the positive state you have induced, ask them to see the image, hear the sound and make the gesture and notice how this brings back the positive feeling. If it does not, ask them to go back more strongly into the experience and set up the associations again. Repeat until these associations or 'anchors' they have set up bring back the positive feeling on their own.

They now have three anchors to use to get into a resourceful state at any time. Ask them to 'practise' using these associations. The more they use them the more quickly and easily they will work. We habitually see and hear things and respond emotionally without thinking. This process is a way of having choice about how you respond emotionally in a given situation.

Finally ask them to imagine going to the examination room or concert hall, opening the door, seeing the examiner or audience, and using their anchors. When the time comes for real, the surroundings will trigger a positive resourceful state rather than an unresourceful one. They are creating the whole experience in their imagination, and feeling resourceful about it. The associations may work well, but you have to remember to use them. Make sure they look as resourceful as they did when they thought back to their positive experience. Performers mentally rehearse their musical performance, this simply extends the idea to the performance context as well.

The most significant difference between an anxious state and a resourceful state is the breathing pattern. A powerful saying I remember in this context is that Anxiety equals excitement minus breathing. An anxious emotional state always goes with a particular breathing pattern. Changing it is the greatest single change you can make to getting into a resourceful state. Make sure you calibrate the resourceful breathing pattern, and make sure this is present when the student mentally rehearses the examination or perform-ance. It is often useful to teach them to do it consciously. Breathing is the point where body and mind link with the music. Breathing relates directly to phrasing the music. We say the music 'breathes', or a performer 'breathes life into the music'. I think these are more accurate metaphors than we might imagine. Music creates tension. Without tension, there can be no resolution. Breathing also creates tension, which is resolved in exhaling.

Bibliography

Posture, tension and instrumental teaching methods are dealt with fully in: **Not Pulling Strings** Joseph O'Connor (*Lambent Books 1987*)

For an excellent book on performance anxiety and how to deal with it, see: **A Soprano on her Head** Eloise Ristad (*Real People Press 1982*)

Notes on the Contributors

Kató Havas is well known on both sides of the Atlantic for her lectures and demonstrations on her teaching methods of string players. She is the author of *A New Approach to Violin Playing, The Twelve Lesson Course, The Violin and I* and *Stage Fright, Its Causes and Cures* (Bosworth and Co. London). She has issued a video – produced by Bill Watkinson Associates, Cumbria – on her 'new approach on the causes and cures of physical injuries in violin and viola playing'.

Vilem Tausky, former Director of Opera at the Guildhall School of Music and Drama, has conducted most of the leading orchestras in Britain and Europe and appeared as guest conductor at Covent Garden and with the English National Opera.

Alfred Nieman, well-known composer, was Professor of Music and Composition at the Guildhall School of Music and Drama. He has lectured on contemporary music, analysis and improvision and trained post-graduate students in improvisation for the Music Therapy Course at the Guildhall School.

Walter Gruner was born in Frankfurt and studied piano, voice and opera production in Frankfurt, Leipzig and Vienna. Closely connected with adult education he lectured at the City Literary Institute for many years. As a professor at the Guildhall School of Music and Drama, he taught voice production and German Lied, in which he was an international authority. He died in 1979.

Leigh Howard was Head of the Department of Speech and Voice at the Guildhall School of Music and Drama. Trained at RADA she spent some years acting in the professional theatre before concentrating on teaching. She became interested in opera, working with singers as director and teacher. For some time she was in charge of speech and dialogue at the London Opera Centre and was a speech coach to the English Music Theatre Company.

Nelly Ben-Or teaches the Alexander Technique at the Guildhall School of Music and Drama, having trained at the Alexander Foundation in London. She is a concert pianist and has appeared as soloist and in chamber music in Europe, Israel, Australia and the United States. She combines her recital work with teaching the piano and giving lectures and workshops in the Alexander Technique.

Carola Grindea was piano professor at the Guildhall School of Music and Drama, also giving courses in 'Techniques of Piano Teaching'. She regularly conducts workshops and gives lecture/demonstrations on 'Tension in Performance' in colleges on both sides of the Atlantic. She is co-director of the Performing Arts Clinic at the London College of Music.

Gervase de Peyer was born in London and studied at the Royal College of Music. He was a founder member of the Melos Ensemble and principal clarinet in the London Symphony Orchestra. In 1969 he joined the Chamber Music Society of the Lincoln Center, New York. He now commutes between Europe and the USA, pursuing an international career as soloist or partiipant in chamber music and, in recent years, also as a conductor.

Dr Paul Lehrer is a clinical psychologist. He is Professor of Psychology at Rutgers College of Medicine and Dentistry, New Jersey, where he directs a clinic that specialises in the treatment of anxiety and tension. Dr. Lehrer has published many studies on the physiological effects of anxiety and various relaxation techniques. He is an international authority on stress and stress management.

Edmund Jacobson was one of the most influential psychologists and physicians of the twentieth century. He was the first to perform scientific studies of the effects of relaxation on human physiology and health. He devised the method of progressive relaxation, described in this volume, which remains the most commonly used relaxation method among clinical specialists in stress management. He conducted experiments on the relationship between muscle activity and mental processes and was one of the first researchers in the field of psychosomatic medicine. He died in 1983 aged 94.

Joseph O'Connor is a guitarist, author and trainer. *Not Pulling Strings* (Lambent Books 1987) explores the psychology of music teaching and learning. *Introducing Neuro-Linguistic Programming* (HarperCollins 1990) deals with excellence in communication. *Listening Skills in Music* (Lambent Books 1989) is a booklet and video on the results of his study into musical talent at the Menuhin School in Surrey. O'Connor is a trainer in communcation skills and music education. He also runs courses in England and Germany on accelerated learning and music.